About the Author

Eric is living in France and pursuing his childhood love of the French language. He loves linguistics, studying foreign languages, and learning so much while teaching English to speakers of other languages. Traveling in Europe and Central Asia has been his amazing experience, and he has seen so much in the past few years. He is thankful to God for the opportunities he has uncovered and for Him still including him in His plan of intellect and discovery in this ever-changing world. He prays more of us are included.

Moving Medusa

Eric Eugene Flannagan Jr

Moving Medusa

Olympia Publishers
London

www.olympiapublishers.com
OLYMPIA PAPERBACK EDITION

Copyright © Eric Eugene Flannagan Jr 2023

The right of Eric Eugene Flannagan Jr to be identified as author of this work has been asserted in accordance with sections 77 and 78 of the Copyright, Designs and Patents Act 1988.

All Rights Reserved

No reproduction, copy or transmission of this publication may be made without written permission.
No paragraph of this publication may be reproduced, copied or transmitted save with the written permission of the publisher, or in accordance with the provisions of the Copyright Act 1956 (as amended).

Any person who commits any unauthorized act in relation to this publication may be liable to criminal prosecution and civil claims for damage.

A CIP catalogue record for this title is available from the British Library.

ISBN: 978-1-80439-031-3

This is a work of creative nonfiction. The events are portrayed to the best of the author's memory. While all the stories in this book are true, some names and identifying details have been changed to protect the privacy of the people involved.

First Published in 2023

Olympia Publishers
Tallis House
2 Tallis Street
London
EC4Y 0AB

Printed in Great Britain

Dedication

To Mark, Bill, and Kip: thank you so much for helping me along the way.

Acknowledgments

Thanks to Brunella for the editing and advice.

MOVING MEDUSA

A MEMOIR ABOUT THE MADISON HOUSE BIG SIBLINGS PROGRAM AND GROWING UP IN CHARLOTTESVILLE

"The act of writing requires a constant plunging back into the shadow of the past where time hovers ghostlike."
— Ralph Ellison

Preface

Kudos to you if you are clever enough to get the play on words when you realize you are reading a preface in a book with Medusa in the title. I hope you are because I decided to write a preface to be this sort of clever. Here I'll be talking about Charlottesville, Virginia, my life growing up around the University of Virginia, and my involvement with Madison House. And in my account of one of the many faces of so-called America the Beautiful, in which I compare her to the presage and pessimism of the exiled Medusa, I hope everything is obvious and that you'll jump off the last page into an admirer's clarity and safely from the scorner's myopic glare.

It took me a few years to finish this as I trudged along after a decade of substance abuse, heavy-headed and hoping for a total recall about my experience with Madison House and its Big Siblings Program as I traveled through Europe and Eurasia. When it occurred to me that I had an interesting story to tell with some interesting and parlayable circumstances, principal characters, and profitable aftermath, I decided to begin. Madison House is the organization at the University of Virginia that coordinates all of the student volunteer efforts in the surrounding Charlottesville community. Despite Madison House being on the UVA campus, it is a non-profit organization that is independent of the university. The memories I have of Madison House are pretty cool and remind me that I am not as empty as I feel. I don't want empty to sound exclusively negative, but I have played host to many an abused substance and my empty is a curious space. The purge and purgatory of emptying are necessary things, in fact, in the sense that one should take the time to empty. Empty is a state and a verb, and over the past few years, I have been looking at myself and what the Big Siblings Program has meant to me, and emptying via the writing process as I somberly approach middle age.

I remember one day my father saw that I was choking on a piece of hot cinnamon candy at CVS drugstore on the Downtown Mall and, in a panic, quickly flipped me upside down, grabbed my ankles, and shook me up and down until the candy was expelled out of my mouth. It wasn't the traditional Heimlich maneuver, but it worked – it felt like shaking an Etch-A-Sketch when you wanted to start over. And writing this has been about as awkward as getting turned upside down by your father and having a hot cinnamon candy disc being dislodged from your throat, and I hope you will respect my personal audit.

Looking around my father's apartments when I was younger, I always saw that he was a writer. I remember I begged and begged him to buy me a set of Encyclopedia Britannicas. I was so young and enamored with the look of them. They looked so perfect on the shelf and the new book smell was nice and gluey. I had no real reason for them; I just wanted them. I remember his corduroy book cover that had a legal notepad with yellow paper where he would jot ideas and begin paragraphs, but there was nothing ever finished. It always looked like the beginning of a memoir, or some attempt to come to terms with himself. I know the frustration of starting to write something but never catching enough incentive to finish it. It is a shame when your body tells you that you don't feel like finishing something you started writing. It feels like what your body won't tell you is the same thing your brain won't say. Fortunately for me, I started writing this and I didn't let myself stop. Fortunately for me, where the sidewalk ends, is where my corduroy road began.

Before the Madison House Big Siblings program, among the first mentor situations I saw was a girl for whom my mother was a mentor, who was named Prentiss. I would see her gait walking beside my mother, like a little apprentice, as I saw my mother see herself in that young girl. I was only six or seven years old and saw that girl and that woman to be some golden ratio, in sync like daughter and mother. Prentiss represented the perimeter of youth over which my mother could never cross again, right there in what was the morbid and pathological geometry of Garrett Square Apartments in Charlottesville. As we all get older, none of us can cross over that perimeter of ours, at least not on this earthly plane. As we move forward in life, it's always just right there a second ago, but no longer in reach. I saw my mother intervening once in an argument between her mentee, Prentiss, and some other neighborhood girls, for which some other adults chastised my mother for engaging with those young girls. She was completely shocked that her maturity was being questioned because she thought she was doing the right thing, but evidently her peers saw a certain lack of objectivity on her part that was not appropriate. I recollect the betrayal and dejection she felt. The dynamic of mentorship was already an in-house thing, as that wasn't the only time I would see my mother humbled-by-committee like that. Those adults who came against my mother's decision to get involved the way she did were a part of our fellowship group in the neighborhood community center there in Garrett Square. An adult showing off in front of children on behalf of another child was not acceptable.

My first Big Brother used to play songs by the band Little

Feat as we rode through Charlottesville doing all kinds of new and exciting things that provided me that particularly optimistic angle and glimpse into adult life. I thought he meant 'feet' when he first told me who they were as we drove off to one of the darkrooms at UVA for him to develop some of his black and white photography. Maybe that quiet insinuation of letting that band play was to disguise him being on his soapbox about the investing of his time on my behalf. Doing things for people makes you proud of yourself. Even in my forties, I meander through all of those synaptic memories of him and my two other Big Brothers, essentially interceding and interjecting on my adolescence as I try to capitulate what type of return an investor of his or her time and money would expect on such an investment.

When you're a little boy or girl and under a mentor's wing like that, you're walking on water. It's such a great feeling being included on a college student's weekly schedule, and being along for the ride as they go about their academic itinerary. Everyone knows how kids put adults on a pedestal. Before God told adults to wash each other's feet, he told children to respect their elders. And unlike him, I had been from a single-parent household. Was he proud about how he was taking his time and doing something nice for someone less fortunate; and if his interest in photography led him to develop the depth of someone's negative circumstances into something glossy and positive? All three of my Big Brothers were mindfully meticulous in their cajoling of my adolescent optimism, and very consistent and punctual while they were in Charlottesville's townie-student diglossia. Did each of my Big Brothers learn from me like I learned from them?

I remember sitting in the passenger seat the first time Mark picked me up from my house on Olinda Drive, thinking of something to say to parlay my timidity into a meaningful contribution to our dialogue, when I asked him who it was playing from his stereo. We often listened to Little Feat on the way to whatever activities he had planned for us. Mark had an invocative photographer's mantra that wasn't so obvious. He always took me along as he worked with negatives, Ilford photo paper, and the developing, stop, and fixer baths. And all my Olan Mills family pictures with my own brothers, each of us laminated and glossy by our own baptism and whole armor of God through life, procured my sense of fraternity through and beyond those photos, still warm with their original colors. All the nagging water under the bridge of the past still babbles past with its divisive prerogative, but the mill and the waterwheel are just up ahead, and I can make the brook work for me.

The situation in Charlottesville with my generation of African American students was particularly delicate to the observer in the late eighties because there was no more debating legislation about our inclusion into full-blown citizenship, but we were all petrified when we saw Emmett Till's open casket and his corpse in the Eyes on the Prize series we were shown at school. His mother wanted everyone to see how those grown, white and narrow-minded men cracked his young black head wide open, so she drew back the curtains and challenged the media. We were so young then during the ebb and flow of the crack epidemic, and Reaganomics in America, and such little wolves about learning. And we had all heard about some Russian lady named Anastasia who was really a princess. We would often see Big Brothers and Big Sisters at our school band performances, plays, and sports matches, shielded from the generation before. We would have never known, sitting among those mostly white UVA students, how our parents were really walking on broken glass while raising us, and how segregation and crack sought to broadly compromise our primordial senses of empathy and human kinship.

That's why it was such news when the white supremacists marched and psychobabbled through the streets of Charlottesville, exalting the Confederacy while Donald Trump was president. They attempted to make it a statutory thing to lobby for equal protection under the Constitution and expected the community to acquiesce to their audacious outburst. And they'll continue to try and dupe atrophy into the Black Power fist, even with less national media attention. Keeping what they consider cognate as a part of black people's historical cognition is their atrocious imperative. They wake up every so often in their algorithm to entice people to look at the shit and expectorant they regurgitate as they insinuate that they bear the burden of some lost legacy. But there are more good people in Charlottesville who are working to harness the narrative and the financial power in the Black Community. That's one of the good things about Charlottesville: there are more good people than bad. And Christians know that God is visiting all the world's generational iniquities, those atrocious and deplorable things that just keep happening, and that He's reacting through the good and emboldened people. You can hear His bassy staccato on the upright June sun rays in America make special and occasional sense of the men and their drums.

My generation is all grown-up now, and some of our parents have died, and some are alive and still in their empty nests without us, and Emmett Till is still the scarecrow in everyone's front yard. We murder and continue to get murdered just like our parents while White and Black America mull and hypothesize the many aftereffects of Jim Crow. More and more blacks skeptically embrace Juneteenth, and we get smeared in the media to the chagrin of Sarah Breedlove because our attention span, our life skills, and our black faces have never been collectively adequate enough to coalesce with said White America.

Charlottesville is a college town inside the Confederate heritage with a world-renowned university that postures for athletes, wealthy families, and anyone who can generate revenue behind a so-called Honor System. At UVA, there is a fine line between failing honorably and having cheated to graduate, with hilarious takes on academic integrity. And African American students have to live with the insinuation that many of us limped into UVA only with the crutch of affirmative action. We are forever attached to the opportunity cost of being black and that which we could have achieved if there had been no slavery and segregation, and we'll probably never escape the cruel experimental psychology of it all.

Exeter Wounds

The day my mom came to the door in her Grateful Dead "dancing bears" t-shirt was the first little exchange between Mark and her that went over my head. When he saw her in it, he reacted with a smile and a rather coy, "Nice shirt." She looked very game to the situation like a Tussaud wax sculpture looks alert and alive, and I knew about her Tussy underarm deodorant she always wore. He stood there ruminating like a young Gregory Peck, tarrying in a blazer, white t-shirt and khakis and showed the ivory breadth of his white teeth. I had no idea who the Grateful Dead were, but I had seen her wear that t-shirt several times while she was cleaning but never made anything of it. Mark and I were standing on the porch right to the left of a bush which some lightning had struck and split its trunk in front of our house on Olinda Drive. My mom was standing in the doorway, blocking the view of the living room and her prized oriental rugs and curios containing her substantial crystal collection. Our living room was for guests and decoration only, and you could clearly see into the house if the curtains were drawn. The window to my room was to the left of the front door. Venetian blinds covered it, and I could see you, but you couldn't see me when I peeked out from my position stage right. My things on my dresser always lay in disarray. Outside of my door, in the hallway and to the left, was the door leading to the basement steps and washroom. And to the right was the kitchen threshold with no door. You could just walk right into the kitchen. I started puberty in that room, and I could knight to the basement or to the kitchen from that room: two steps forward and one step to the left or right from the foot of my bed.

Mark was my Big Brother from Madison House at the University of Virginia who had come to be my friend and mentor for the year. I had requested a Big Brother while I was at Jackson-Via Elementary School. I was nine years old and in the fourth grade. I thought to myself that it would be a cool thing for me to do. Madison House is an independent volunteer center for students at the University of Virginia on Rugby Road in Charlottesville, Virginia, right near Beta Bridge. The Big Siblings program beckoned, and I crossed over to another side of life in my hometown. My fourth-grade homeroom and science teacher, Mrs. Harding, told us about the Madison House Big Siblings program as she blinked behind her big rose-colored bifocals. She said that we could have the opportunity to be Little Brothers or Little Sisters in the program if we wanted. She read from some notes of which she was in possession as we were all ears. I quickly computed what the Little Sibling-Big Sibling relationship would be like, and I was immediately interested and adroitly signed up on the paper she passed around for those students who were curious.

I, a Virginian from most modest and government-assisted beginnings, would be matched with a lanky white Connecticuter from a family with money the following school year after summer vacation. I have always assumed the pairing process was just a gut feeling that some person who worked there had, or something alphabetical. I didn't actually know how matching interested Little Siblings with available Big Siblings worked then, some thirty-five years ago. I was paired with Mark and Kip, my first and third Big Brothers, via whatever this algorithm had been. My second Big Brother, Bill, and Mark were close friends who went to Phillips Exeter Academy in New Hampshire, and there was a quiet and subtle changing of the guard when Mark asked Bill to be my new Big Brother as Mark was about to graduate. Kip had no connection to Mark or Bill. Back then, it didn't seem that people expected white males to step up and face what went on in the country like they do now. People expect them to step up and be a part of the change these days. Something so simple as taking a couple of hours a week to go to the movies, go get ice cream, go to a museum, or go play basketball or soccer can make such a big difference.

Bill studied Russian and was very much in love with his girlfriend, and future wife, Amy. (Bill and Amy had two children together, I have seen via Facebook, but Amy passed away.) I remember when I first saw Amy and thought that she was the most beautiful woman I had ever seen. If she had wanted to date me back then, I would have definitely been open to the idea, even though I was only eleven or twelve. One day, while we were walking past Mad Bowl, Mark saw Bill and started talking with him as I listened along. We were almost directly across from the Fralin Museum of Art. Bill took out a folded piece of paper from his pocket with a diamond engagement ring that he had had specially crafted for Amy. Mark was still my Big Brother through Madison House, but upon his exit from UVA and subsequent move to Taiwan to teach English and be an investment banker, this chapter of Mark's and my relationship would end as he would go off to become successful in the world of finance and internet consulting. I remember I cried and cried for days after Mark left to begin the next chapter of his life.

Bill was much more reserved than Mark and less into drinking. Bill's sister was dating Mark's housemate, Mark, who everyone called "Killer Bee". He and Sally went on to get married. I thought this was odd because Killer Bee was a weird dude. One day, he told me that if I were ever to save my belly button lint, give it to him because he was in the process of making a sweater from his own belly button lint, and he could really use mine, especially if I wasn't going to do anything with it. I think he went to Exeter, too. Bill did what Mark did. I had already known Bill from hanging out at the SPE fraternity house where Mark used to live during our first year hanging out together. Bill took me out to places and let me hang out at his house. His interest in Russian influenced me one summer as I would go to the Virginia Governor's Language Academy to study French. I had the opportunity to explore a second foreign language. I chose Russian and was taught by a short, black woman from Madagascar, the furthest thing I expected to see when thinking of Russian teachers.

I would go over to Bill's house and do my homework and get tutoring and other advice. It was somewhere that I could get away from my house for a while. I could always count on pointers for writing assignments or help with other assignments, and a quiet sanctuary-like place to study. I guess the goal here was to ensure my safe keeping, despite Mark's physical absence in my life, as we would continue to correspond over the coming years. Mark spent a lot of time in China and Taiwan and would regularly send me airmail letters and little cultural ornaments that I would proudly put amongst my mother's haul.

Kip was the athlete of the three. He looked just like the actor James Caan. Kip loved to play basketball, and we often went to Forest Hills Park near where I lived, and he would show me how he could dunk. We would play two-on-two games against neighborhood kids, and I would be proud of my white-boy partner. He was white and could jump, which shattered such a significant nineties' stereotype. Kip's real name was Kipling, like

Rudyard Kipling's last name, the British poet who wrote the poem "The White Man's Burden", encouraging U.S. imperialism. Kip's dunking ability was what I remember about him, as he would often impress with behind-the-back lobs to himself and then jam it home. We did the same manner of things as Mark and Bill, just more locally based. I never went anywhere out of the city with Kip. Our visits tended to be close to my house. Kipling's entry into my life makes my Madison House story pretty neat and intriguing. It's a perfect segue into the question of people's motivation and psychology when interacting with others from different walks of life. Colonialism and imperialism were huge deals in world history. The commonwealth of Virginia and Thomas Jefferson's university have a permanent connection with the two that should never be erased.

The primary drafter of the Declaration of Independence is the ghost-in-residence of my hometown. He is still the posthumous antagonizer in the debate about social injustice. And James Monroe's Ash Lawn plantation is only two miles away from Monticello. America evolved from isolationism to imperialism a little more than a century after it declared independence from Britain and found itself enriched by quite a haul after the Spanish-American War and the Treaty of Paris. Then, the exceptional white Americans would use the Monroe Doctrine to put the major world powers on notice by saying that any attempt to expand spheres of influence into Latin America would be considered acts of aggression against the United States, and that the 'open door policy' regarding China should have been consolation enough for the other world powers while the United States bullied its way through Central America and the Caribbean in the Banana Wars with Manifest Destiny as the rationale.

In the last few years, as the United States has become

increasingly under the microscope for White Privilege and the legacy of disenfranchisement White Privilege has created in the African American community, you can hear how black people are increasingly reminding whites that their silence about current and past injustice is just as bad as the injustice itself. We blacks have always lived in this shadow of White Privilege. I think today's generation has no problem seeing it and understanding its effects on our career development and family life, but the thing that bites is having to dignify it with a response. I was fortunate enough to have a very enriching experience with Madison House, and the way I see it is just that: the way I see it.

I presume Madison House to be named after Dolley Madison. The first First Lady, whose famous parties hosted both the Democratic and Republican Parties in the name of what we know today as bipartisan politics, was the wife of the fourth President, James Madison. Together, they owned Paul Jennings, author of the first memoir about life in the White House, and lived civilian life on the Montpelier plantation in Orange County, Virginia, which is about a half-hour drive from Charlottesville. I compile my everyday life according to my involvement with Madison House. It was a life-changing experience. My life has been a book in the making because of the Big Siblings program: a unique story about the church, public school, black and white, introversion, obstacles, and boundaries. I have had to make myself backtrack along the divide of my life that lies between what it was like to grow up in my mother's household and what it would have been like growing up in a household with both my mother and my father.

Pondering people's entries and exits in my life, pulling the memories from the darkroom in my head, and arranging the images into a narrative is particularly aggravating at times. Had

I never attempted to piece all of the memories together and made my conclusions about myself as an adult and all that constituted my maturation, or appreciated the grace that allowed me to sit here today and be able to say it honestly and clearly, perhaps I would have never understood how necessary it has been for people to leave this kind of evidence of their personal reconciliations. It has been years since I have had any kind of writing class, but I remember a lot from the writing classes I had, and I usually remember most of my interactions with people. I think the interactions I had with my three Big Brothers were important for my development as a person. I spend a lot of time scavenging for details, and I worry a little when I don't remember everything. Turning those details into an examination of my behavior and turning that examination of my behavior into an explanation of where I am from and who my parents are is a recognition of the past that has a lot to do with restful nights and peace of mind during a day of work and errands. So, I need to remember them, and the need is primordial. It's my responsibility to make my life matter now. Making my life matter can mean building a reputation, planning for the future and other lives I potentially become responsible for, which doesn't have to be strictly confined to the life or lives that I create, and offering my experiences as empathy. There must be so many stories about the Big Siblings program, and I am only one perspective from a unique set of circumstances.

A Bipolar Boy

The flash of a polaroid commemorated me as one of several people who were voted "most likely to succeed" from Buford Middle School by my peers when I was thirteen years old. I had been involved with the Big Siblings program for the third year at that point. We were seventh and eighth graders in that school, and we were preparing for high school. I remember I had on my best shirt in that picture with the others. It was a button-up dress shirt with thin, vertical stripes of dark colors, and I had on some black pants because I knew we would be taking pictures because we superlative winners had already been notified.

I hadn't gotten a haircut for some reason the weekend before, so my hair was unkempt for failure to get my usual biweekly coif. I always hated walking around without a fresh haircut. I shuddered to think what the shutter would capture as it blinked, so I kept patting my hair down throughout that morning because I knew how the day was going to go. My nervous and dejected patting was reluctance to take that picture; moreover, I ended up in the middle of the group, cast to the center of the photo. I actually had no idea that my peers at school thought that highly of me. I was very surprised when I heard that I had been voted as a person most likely to succeed. I wasn't really that popular. I felt haunted at that school from not winning the spelling bee either of the years that I was there. That was more damning than distinguishing, and I was going to be leaving soon. It could have been worse because I was only there for two years, but it felt like it just kept happening.

It was so embarrassing to lose, but it happened anyway. When I lost in eighth grade, I remember storming back to my classroom, fully electric with anger and not wanting to be bothered by anyone. Just as I was comfortable in not wanting to be bothered, there came April, my white-girl crush, further raining on my pity party and telling me that everything would be okay. I had no desire to hear any words of encouragement, and Ms. Catlin knew it, leading her to catch eyes with April and shake her head 'no', as in to say that now was not the time. I had again built my hopes up to win the spelling bee, and they had come crashing down again, just like the year before. When it rained, it poured, and I exited middle school plagued by a worrisome mediocrity. April, I, and a small group of other students were in the Quest program in the Charlottesville City Schools that encouraged skepticism among the students, in that we were gently warned about accepting things the way they are. We had been warned about the vanity of face value. I had been in the Quest program since elementary school. We were invited to challenge opinions because we were the students who would go on to change things in the world with the critical thinking skills we practiced week to week.

The general idea behind the program was to encourage students to take risks in their writing and in their application of the scientific method. It encouraged students to challenge ideas and to think outside the box. We did a lot of unique problem-solving involving science and math, and maybe we were even a part of an early root system that gave way to the STEM (science, technology, engineering, and mathematics) program we see in education today. Quest was one day a week throughout the school year, and this program distinguished us from other students in the school. We were really a select few relative to the grade we were in, and we didn't have to attend regular classes while we were in Quest. Sometimes we would get called to the school auditorium on the intercom system, and everyone else would just look as we, the students in the Quest program, got up and proceeded to the auditorium. Each grade up until high school had this select few students who were in the Quest program.

People have accused the Quest paradigm of structural bias in that it has been a program designed to segregate the less gifted black students from the more gifted whites by condoning a certain amount of gifted black students to mingle with the gifted whites. If you research the history of the Quest program, you will find that it has come under much criticism for racial disparities, the earliest controversy being as an early state resistance to federal desegregation efforts. More and more integration was happening in the Charlottesville public schools to the chagrin of many area whites in the late 1950s after the Brown vs. Topeka Board of Education decision in 1954. So, a local lady proposed that there be a program that the highest-achieving white students could test into, also allowing for a small percentage of blacks. This was the plan to limit desegregation and intermingling of the races. Twenty years later, the Quest program was started in 1976, almost identical to the woman's proposal. I always felt like I was on an island in the Quest program. I knew that the program was a good thing, and I really felt lucky to be a part of it, and I looked forward to the activities and curriculum we did, but I always felt alone. Sometimes it was a nagging loneliness that reminded me I was a minority, and other times it was a healthy solitude where I felt rewarded, and I was figuring out what I was good at.

I was born out of wedlock in 1978, the product of separated parents who found out the burden of truth about unplanned parenthood. My two older brothers were from my mother's first marriage, and my father's pack-of-mayonnaise-white new college student and waitress girlfriend from Mahopac also worked at Planned Parenthood. This is a crude and short-sighted mnemonic to describe Linda's origin and first appearance in my life, but I had no problem at all with Linda. I thought she was cool, but life always reminded me that my parents didn't plan for me. As Mom had been losing her footing and sometimes dreading the chore of having me around, Dad had been gaining traction, shedding his skin and wriggling free from preconceived notions about race and relationships. For six years, until my first little brother was born, it was just me and my mother living together, canvassing the system for food stamps and other social services, and anticipating child support checks via the commonwealth of Virginia from the labor of this black man with an Irish last name. I imagine I had been just fine in the amniotic commonwealth in her belly. But gestation ran its course, and I came out into light and vaccinations in my butt, demanding nutrition and attention. I found my way out of the hole and among the general population, a great and delicious unplanned burden for her.

My father and I were such polar opposites in dimension and theory: he was big, and I was little (he was Big Eric, and I was Little Eric). I was already Little Eric before I was a Little Sibling. My father was a bold drum major who never finished high school, yet I was a reluctant clarinetist woodwinder being groomed for college. I had originally wanted to play saxophone and become a famous jazzman, but renting the saxophone was too expensive for my mother, so my cousin let me have her old clarinet. My father's resume was a long scroll of restaurant experience as he meandered from job to job. He always talked about starting his own restaurant, some small type of bistro, but he never did. He lived and worked in Blacksburg, Virginia, the home of the Virginia Tech Hokies, and I always ventured into enemy territory every summer in Blacksburg beneath the Chicago maroon and burnt orange banners and pennants of Virginia Tech. One of the big game days in Charlottesville is when UVA plays Virginia Tech, or formally Virginia Polytechnic Institute and State University, or just 'Tech' for short. Blacksburg was a dream to explore, and I was always completely secure that I was a visitor there and that I was from rival Charlottesville. I used to wake up from my nap in the backseat near the transmission to the déjà vu of Blacksburg after the three-hour drive down I-81 from Charlottesville to southwest Virginia. I woke up ready for fun times and no schoolwork. Then the dream ended every late August when I had to come home. The same socio-economic dynamic that exists between Charlottesville and the University of Virginia exists between Blacksburg and Virginia Tech University. Their communities are structured around universities that are marketable for academics and athletics.

My dad always watched, camouflaged in the reds and browns of autumn, sipping Milwaukee's Best, as I had just exited Blacksburg after charming and heroic summers where he knew he was the protagonist. He slid and glided off to work and back every day during the summer, making soups, appetizers, and entrées, consistently smithing this remote identity I knew that supported his child a few hours north up interstate 81. I came knocking every summer, but only with permission from the woman he knocked up because he didn't have any real custody of me. He always called me 'King Tut', and I came to know how he invisibly handed my mom those child support checks while his photographer, and Kodak store clerk girlfriend Linda was there to document it all at Lantern Ridge and Ridgeview apartments in Blacksburg. We all lived together with Gorba and Raisa, her two cats named after Mikhail Gorbachev and his wife, Raisa. Gorba had a patch of discolored fur on her forehead, in the same place as Mikhail Gorbachev's birthmark. I always used to thumb through her photo albums, and she would always take pictures of us three during our bourgeois summer shenanigans in Blacksburg. She also interpreted it all with her sketchbooks and cray-pas, as her photos and artwork together were worth thousands upon thousands of words. She was a jill of many trades, and they had met while working at the same restaurant as she was moonlighting. I used to watch my dad's older brother, my uncle William, slide and glide, too, as he entered and exited. The only difference was that Uncle William worked nights, yet his nickname was Sunnyboy. He would leave his house on Camellia Drive and go to work at night at the Ix building in Charlottesville, Virginia. He always rode his ten-speed bicycle to work after dinner, and my cousin and I would see his long legs lazily pedaling in one of the easy gears upstream, up the slight incline toward Willoughby and 5th Street Extended. I was so little then and wondered how his legs could be so long. He blocked the moon when he stood up straight, and my cousin Alex and I watched from the window or the front yard as he disappeared up the street.

Language Arts and the Hideously Loaded Question

During my first meeting with my faculty advisor at UVA, the labor historian Dr. Nelson Lichtenstein, he told me that he was doing research about the Ix company. I remember how I had wandered over to that meeting with him, ready to toot my own horn with my black boy magic in hand, in my very own 'nuit américaine', my first important meeting with a faculty member at UVA who shared the same name as the Lichtenstein near Germany and among the teutophones, and who must have only been there during his Guggenheim Fellowship. I have only a vague recollection of our exchange, and I never thought I would make a connection with that meeting with him so much later in my life. Each advisor has their own constellation of students in front of whom said advisor rotates, and the psychological probe of UVA life had begun from this faculty member and his off-campus interests. I don't think I ever told Dr. Lichtenstein about my involvement with Madison House, but I think he had been made aware that I was from Charlottesville.

The Frank Ix and Sons textile company used to be right across from South First Street housing projects on Elliott Avenue and Rayon Street. I have lived along the Silk Road in Central Asia in what was the Soviet Union, and I remember learning how the blasphemy of communism used to loom and hover, so ghostlike, over American political and social thought. It was the proverbial gun to the head of capitalism and the shame of right-wing politics. Now all those lessons about McCarthyism and the Cuban Missile Crisis, the Cold War, and rumors of Russian espionage and hacking float around in the ethereal post-data of old propaganda and smear journalism.

   A few years ago, I decided to move to Kazakhstan to learn Russian after I had been learning the Croatian language and culture in the former Yugoslavia in Zagreb. Living in newly independent republics, formerly parts of two separate confederations, was a counterintuitive experience for me because I am from the United States. I learned to embrace what was counterintuitive because real life was more than my previous local existence in Charlottesville. I was just starting to overcome the language barrier of Croatian before I decided to move to Kazakhstan to learn Russian. These were two Slavic languages, yet I had only learned Romance languages up to that point. Croatia had a much easier visa process because it was virtually nonexistent. Once I learned that I didn't need to apply for a long-stay visa in Croatia as long as I was studying the language or had a job, I signed up for intensive introductory Croatian classes at the University of Zagreb, and I studied Croatian for a year. I would have continued had I not decided to move to Central Asia. The "Z" in Zagreb makes me think of the Z Society symbols people see around grounds at UVA.

   A few months before my move to Kazakhstan, after a conversation about a job opportunity in Georgia by the Black Sea with my cousin Kiara, I decided to go and work in Shekvetili, Georgia, at an English-speaking summer camp for kids who wanted to learn English. When that summer ended, I also decided that learning Russian would help me become a better version of myself. The Silk Road had come calling, and I would know two Slavic languages, which could only be a good thing. Most of the organizers of this program in Georgia were from Kazakhstan, so I figured I would go there and have a few friends around. I was going to immerse myself in the former Soviet Union to speak Russian. After overstaying my one-month tourist visa in Kazakhstan, going to court and paying lawyer fees and a fine, I discovered Bishkek, Kyrgyzstan was just a short hour-and-a-half flight away from Nur Sultan, and the cost of living was cheaper. There was also a two-month tourist visa period, and the winters were milder for a hermetic like myself.

I don't know what my uncle did at the Ix building back in those days. I was more preoccupied with the fact that it was a night job. My uncle Sunnyboy worked the graveyard shift and returned from the dead every morning just as it was time for me and my cousins, Alex and Junebug (who was really William, Jr.), to go to school. I stayed at my uncle's house on the weekends a lot when I was young, and my mom wanted to go to the Odyssey nightclub with her nieces.

The Ix company was a textile mill that began its history in Charlottesville as a silk mill. Frank Ix emigrated from Germany with a few looms and an assignment with another company in the late eighteen hundreds. All five of his sons would come to join him in the textile industry under his namesake, hence the name Frank Ix and Sons. Two of his sons were named William and Alex. By the time World War II started, silk became less and less practical to produce in Virginia because the silk often spoiled en route to Europe, where it was used to help the Allied Forces. The Ix company started to experiment with synthetic fibers and became the world's number one producer of sailing fabrics for a while. The Ix company also made parachutes for humans and supplies during the war.

The mill provided jobs to many Charlottesville residents and was the motivation for a lot of housing development in the surrounding area. To make getting to work easier, the mill also built houses for the employees near the property on nearby streets like Rayon Street to maintain morale, encourage comradery, and for quicker access to shifts because the mill was open every day. But foreign clothes and textiles became much cheaper at the end of the twentieth century, and the factory came to a grinding halt. During its existence, Frank Ix and Sons wove many narratives for Charlottesville and connected it to other parts of the world.

King Cotton's labor-intensive regime of picking and separating cotton by hand had evolved after the invention of the cotton gin in 1793. Now people could work smarter, not harder. After Eli Whitney's invention, cotton became a cash crop until the boll weevil almost destroyed the cotton industry in the 1920s, right before the Great Depression. Whenever I stayed at my uncle William's house, my aunt Veronica always laid out mine and Alex's clothes on Sunday nights for school on Monday morning, and we always saw my uncle just getting home from work on his way to his cocoon-like room to sleep. We usually wore denim jeans, cotton shirts and socks. We knew to avoid going in his room because it always smelled like farts. Alex and I always took turns whenever we had to go wake up Uncle William for dinner.

Frank Ix had left Germany and come to the United States to take advantage of the new ethos of the whites-only American Dream. Here he could own a home, raise a family, and apply his brainstormed ideas to a global vision to establish real upward mobility and generational wealth for his family, and jobs for locals. The California Gold Rush and Manifest Destiny through the midwestern frontier were the beginning movements that would give birth to the American Dream. And the once-isolationist United States would ultimately subscribe to the idea of the White Man's Burden and the notion that it was really the white man's responsibility, in all the glory of this newfound American Dream and superiority, to civilize all the non-white people of the world during the age of European imperialism. Rudyard Kipling encouraged the United States to adopt this philosophy of extending its power and influence through colonization, military force, and evangelical Christianity. It was specifically an encouragement to the United States to further its interests in the Philippines and Guam, but in the Charlottesville City school system, we learned the White Man's Burden was supposed to apply to people of African descent.

Rudyard Kipling claimed the process of civilizing the non-white people of the world had been part of the duty of the British empire and would be necessary for the United States to emerge as a true international powerhouse. His poem was an encouragement to White America to get involved in international affairs because the non-white people, incapable of self-government, inherently inferior, and incapable of improvement, needed civilization. Fast forward a couple hundred years, and we have structural bias and institutional racism. These two phrases diverge from this concept of inherent inferiority as the intrusive White Man's Burden became justifiable. The ramifications of such an idea have created generations of questionable precedents, compromised identities, and strange politics, and the devil is in the details.

Both my parents were born in 1955, just a year after the Brown v. Board of Education ruling passed. Ruby Bridges was just a year older than them. Both were only two or three when Orval Faubus used the Arkansas National Guard to stop the Arkansas Nine from attending Little Rock Central High School. Both were kids during those few years of eternity of state resistance to the Supreme Court's decision about integrating schools. It seems like both my parents purposely abridged their childhood narratives as they were just narrowly included in the omnibus of American history and civics as legal and integrated.

Being smart was something new for me when I was young, but it was not a new thing in the scope of my community. We watched as drugs and alcohol cracked the armor of the Black Community. And the adults knew that drugs and alcohol diluted us. I grew to notice I was usually the only black kid in my class, or one of a few. And that among the black kids in the other classes where that wasn't the case, I usually scored in some top tier of the students. It's fair to say that we black kids wondered what it would have been like to live and learn without that smoggy stigma of being niggers. My parents and their friends loved when I made the honor roll or got accepted into some program that involved academic achievement. It made my parents and their friends feel better; presumably, it was some attempt at closure because of what they had endured a generation before. I used to look at my mom's old high school yearbooks and hear occasional anecdotes from my dad, but they didn't share much with me from those times, so I didn't know much. The older people just smiled and told me how good what I had done was and sometimes gave me money. My mother had had her eyes set on a liberal arts degree before she decided to get married and have a family instead of going to the University of Virginia on a scholarship. Sarah Jackson, my mother, loved to sing and everyone would ask her to sing a solo whenever we went to different churches, and she would always sing solos at our home churches. She loved French in high school but does not remember much of it. I wonder if she would have gone on to major in it at UVA? Just some thirty years before, in 1935, Alice Jackson had been denied entry into the UVA Master's program in French because of her skin color and "for other good and sufficient reasons not necessary to be herein enumerated". Walter Ridley and Gregory Swanson were already in the midst of their professional careers as they had become pioneers at the University of Virginia in the fifties and made it over to the other greener side of the old segregation law. Getting accepted into college for black women was a significantly rarer thing back in the seventies than it is now. UVA did not begin admitting women in general until after 1970. There must have been a lot of pressure involved with committing to such a place and would have been quite a revolutionary step for her at such a time.

In 1987, Monticello and the University of Virginia's Academical Village was named a UNESCO World Heritage Site. This was around the same time I got involved with Madison House. UNESCO World Heritage Sites are chosen because they "represent a masterpiece of human creative genius" and "exhibit an important interchange of human values". Collective white conscience is eased, and countless egos are stroked with every new admission of a black undergraduate at the University of Virginia, especially a new Wahoo on an athletic scholarship. You either resent that part of the process, or you don't. People love UVA and the Hoos, and people want to come to Mr. Jefferson's University. Maybe you have heard the iconoclast's tale about how UVA rejected Dr. Seuss, who in turn built a house on a hill near UVA so he could survey all of Whoville. You can see it in the storyline of 'How the Grinch Stole Christmas', perhaps Theodore Seuss Geisel's most famous book about a fictional town called Whoville, and in the prior book, 'Horton Hears a Who!' It is an achievement if you are black and get accepted into UVA.

The gray area of trying to fit in and be social, maybe keeping a job and studying simultaneously, seeking to do extracurricular things, and dealing with other curves that life can throw at you can be unsettling. Every new admission is another chance to peck at the order of things in America and try to fuse more and more integrity into the black self-image. But not enough black students ever reach the point of realizing that their stories are important and worth communicating to others because we are still relatively new to the academic side of things at Predominantly White Institutions (PWIs) because of White Privilege. More of us need to tell our stories to have more data to address such a question of psychology as black relevance.

Why was I accepted to the University of Virginia? Was I a part of some quota obligation that the federal government mandated? I didn't conventionally succeed there. How much did White Privilege and preference have to do with it? Over the years, these have been among the several questions that keep surfacing in my life. Being an area minority kid was definitely an inside track to admission because there was a recruitment push back then for talented students of color, especially to study engineering. There was the National Society of Black Engineers (NSBE), the Southeastern Consortium for Minorities in Engineering (SECME), and the Summer High School Academic Reach Up Program (SHARP). These were all programs I was a part of growing up in the Charlottesville Public School system. It was like a gate opened, and more of us were welcomed. I always knew that I was an advanced student in grade school, so people always touted me to be a leader. I had role models that I emulated, yet my father didn't raise me day to day. I knew the things I was good at, and I knew I was paying attention for the most part, but I was part of a process bigger than myself. I was a part of a process where black people were emerging from this condition of feeling inferior and beneath whites, yet an onus to be decent and obedient was just in my nature.

I knew there was a power in the pen and with words and that writing could distinguish you from the rest of the pack. It was distinguishing me, and I was learning fundamental things about the writing process. I could just never seem to win the spelling bee. Writing is a process, and great works of fiction, drama, memoir, and biography don't just magically happen. My pen was plugged into my head, but the circuit was breaking because I couldn't get free from what my community was. My community was about the dead-end of substance abuse. Whether I liked it or not, I was from that cycle, that cycle from which I could not ebb. I was from those ephemeral and euphoric highs, yet bottomless and brooding lows. People my age are the generation after the generation that saw the end of the 'separate but equal' era, so there are still triggers in the American system designed to cause confusion and breaches in communication between us two generations. The breach between father and son caused by segregation and White Privilege in the form of the grandfather clauses: the former provision in lawmaking that made a law only applicable to future generations, while some conditions stayed the same in existing situations is a part of the heritage of the United States and makes the question of empathy between me and my parents' generation centrally relevant yet impossible, as the rest of the world seems to be confused by what sympathy and empathy actually are.

Examining and speaking against that spirit of division and rejection that existed in this relatively recent period of American history, where black people actually have civil rights, is important. The confusion that it has caused for my generation has incubated into other critical divisions and problems within families, religion and the church, the workplace, and also global stereotypes about African American men. In his famous debate with William Buckley in 1965, Harlemite James Baldwin called the central question of whether or not the American Dream was at the expense of the American negro "hideously loaded". Of course, the answer is obvious, but he took the time to declare his answer eloquently and show that he had done due diligence to the question, as he summarily reviewed national race relations. He said that he felt like the prophet Jeremiah among the Cambridge student body. He artistically escaped the gruesome question about the paradigm of slavery, inside the continuum of theocratic colonial theory and practice, toward the advent of civil rights for all with the smart and obvious answer: that negroes had been beneath whites and, simultaneously, the foundation of American labor since the slave trade, having been the primary reason for the existence of the ports, harbors, and railroads. And they were this, step by step, while witnessing the violation of their women and the murder of their children. So to escape this status into a social and spiritual coherence through the web of White Privilege was a unique dilemma because the country was not facing what it had done.

I had always figured that finding a way out was what language arts and creative writing were for. That fork in the road where practice diverges from theory was often where you became prey to your own self-destructive psychology, and you realized how hypocritical the white people who governed you were. And you also found out that intelligence can make a lot of enemies. Finding a way out of what your current state of mind had become because of that, or where your head was at or had been, was the pathway to being intellectual. I think both my mother and father understood the future complexities that lay on the pathway on which walked my then narrow behind. For it to be such an umbrella term, I only understood the decided breadth of language arts as reading, composition, speaking, and listening until after I began traveling and became an EFL teacher to finance my adventure. I always knew that part of elementary school was just English class, even though it was called language arts. We learned how to read and how to write. We learned when to say the parts of speech and when and how to be polite. The artistic part would come later with the composition of stories, poems, and plays. It was more than just reading the stories. It was about acting, rhyme, storytelling, and engaging and identifying with consequence. It was also about understanding the authors and their circumstances, so I came to find out. Language arts were the logical way of allowing the tao of critical thinking to help us understand history and modern times. Yet that odd and intimidating barrier of legal segregation in the United States had come and gone by the time I was born. Living and learning were becoming about as easy as realizing you lost your head, but you were ironically sitting on it. As clever as my black generation was allowed to be, we weren't there during our black parents' and grandparents' childhoods, and our parents wanted to see an unadulterated manifestation of living and learning in their children.

We who had no such tangible experience in any time period where it was legal to segregate us had no empathy for our parents. There was only sympathy for them from the whites who actually felt sorry for them from afar and knew that was wrong or who joined them in protest. That structural bias and that institutional racism were centuries-old ghosts that our parents' generation was always busy sniffing out in front of their offspring. They were always busy distancing themselves from it. They were cleaning the kitchen and Electrolux-ing the floor. Their heads were pointed down and focused on finishing, doing things right, and putting this reorientation into perspective. They were buying living room suits and occasional curios and oriental rugs and fans to tuxedo and cool the living room. They were buying patio furniture and outdoor grills to attract and keep people's company and change the black kaleidoscope. They saw more and more life capable in their dark selves and peers, which dilated their pupils so today we can fit more montage than ever inside our line of sight. I was just there because I had just so happened to be there and happened to be a witness to the brew I was seeing. Why I can apply my hindsight to my analysis of the impressionable me from back then began with these exiting ghosts of segregation, Mr. Crow and "separate but equal", who skedaddled off and onward like a couple of ravens. Our parents were trying to make those exit wounds as camouflaged as possible. Now, "back then" has come from out of nowhere to surge into the lead at this theoretical halfway point in my life, and there I am, not so guilty, not so tolerated, not so out of sorts, and not so fast-tracked. There I was back then, a life – this new life. There was space for me to be and see me in my parents' lives because this sore, then scab, then keloid of segregation, had been surgically removed from America the Beautiful's beautiful face.

Through the lenses of my faith and history, I look at my life and my face wrapped around my sinuses. Since God breathed life into Adam, formed from clay, and created an animated man, history has been a coefficient of faith. The evidence of things unseen and documentation of things that have happened both share the substance of things hoped for. As ambiguous as that is, people all around the world are learning from history. Some people are learning to change trends. Some people are learning to exploit them. Any sort of establishing yourself as upwardly mobile and relevant in today's world definitely takes a measure of faith. Some battles you win. Some battles you lose. Sometimes you get credit. Sometimes you don't. Sometimes you deserve credit. Sometimes you don't.

So, I am justified by my faith yet responsible for learning and referencing history. Winston Churchill and George Orwell both said history was written by the winners. They meant the winners of wars. People are always warned that those who make the crucial mistake of not knowing their history will be doomed to repeat it. I am from Charlottesville, Virginia where the educated neo-Nazis live, and statues of Confederate war heroes remind the world of the prosody of slavery, yet used to stand prominently preserved downtown, right in the historical center of the city. Every day people see that their attempt to "unite the right" comes against more and more opposition.

In our world, where stories, land, legacy, and heirlooms are passed down from generation to generation, these statues were part of what it means to live in and be from Charlottesville, Virginia. A lot of households celebrate the Southern Confederacy and also pledge allegiance to white nationalism. Virginia is as central to the Confederate legacy as any other southern state, perhaps even simultaneously the keystone to the Confederacy and the United States. Every American history book points to Jamestown, Virginia, and 1607 as the starting point for the dynamic New World theocratic colonialism in North America. Though in the United States we separate church and state, the nationalists are tickled to death at the irony of the priority given to their First Amendment rights.

The Puritan escape from the religious persecution of Kings

James and Charles would happen in Massachusetts and New Hampshire. New England became a hub for denominational Christianity, and territorial Puritans became as intolerant as the Anglican Church from which they had fled. Meanwhile, the modern capitalist lust for profit in the economy of supply and demand would be leveraged on African knees and backs in Virginia. Release the hounds and chase away the indigenous Native Americans to make way for the surrogate Africans and cotton and indigo and tobacco. For these scarecrows, the cotton was their hair, the indigo became their blues, and the ready-to-sell tobacco was their skin.

The literature we had been given in school growing up contained only an occasional autobiography about the experience of being black in America. By the time we finished high school, we had all read Frederick Douglass's autobiography, and we knew about Malcolm X's, but not everyone had read it. And among the first things we learned in elementary school was that Harriet Tubman led slaves to freedom and that Madame C.J. Walker invented makeup and became a millionaire because of it. Now we could be functional yet cosmetic among our own. We learned that George Washington Carver discovered crop rotation. We knew that it was Rosa Parks who refused to sit in the back of the bus just because she didn't feel like it. It was important that we knew that she just didn't feel like doing that at that particular moment in time. We learned that Dr. Charles Drew made the first blood bank and that Paul Robeson was a mindful force in the theater. Mary McLeod Bethune was a pioneer in educating blacks, and we knew that Booker T. Washington supported vocation, but W.E.B. Du Bois supported education. This was how we learned that things could be mutually exclusive.

It was that dichotomy between vocation and education back

then that was just enough to encourage a person like myself that intelligence was possibly a high road out of that bleak and repulsive history that was the black experience: crime, gangs, prison, disease, depression, untimely death, or life in some form of international exile. Black folklore had painstakingly evolved in front of a white culture that both manufactured it and looked at it as inferior. But at least the stories we heard about black leaders were helping us to trust our own experiences. We were starting to understand and trust our own descriptions of our reality.

I started to learn that the black reality was stolen around the age of twelve or thirteen. The black identity was compromised due to centuries of systematic oppression of black people, and the color of our skin played a role in how we were perceived. And that as we were present here in America, we were absent in the original countries we came from, and robbed of any dividend from that coherence of African sovereignty. It kept some doors open, but it kept others closed. I did not have any authority to interrogate anyone about involvement in the compromising of the black identity through ramifications of slavery, Jim Crow segregation, and other legally justified aggressions, nor did I know that my soul was on ice. Soul on Ice is a collection of essays that Eldridge Cleaver wrote while in Folsom State prison in the 1960s. Cleaver was in and out of reform schools as a child for his repeated involvement in criminal activity. I read those essays when I was twenty while I was living in San Francisco, just across the Bay Bridge from Oakland, the same Oakland where he and the Black Panthers ambushed some Oakland Police Department officers just a few days after James Earl Ray shot Martin Luther King, Jr. in Memphis. That book was a commentary on Black America and the stand-off with US politics back then for civil rights. It helped me realize that who I had been while growing up needed more explanation from investigation, and that the things that had happened in the past set the scene for the things happening in the present.

My family, and families like mine, were a part of the ghetto and a part of rural Virginia. Go to Louisa County, Virginia around the rock quarry, and you will be on my family's land. My parents' generation started in the surrounding counties of the greater Charlottesville area farming, then wound up in Charlottesville working as cooks and nurses, then on to being clerks in human resources departments and electricians and general laborers at the University of Virginia. This had been the difficult and unilateral and serpentine yet labyrinthine climb of upward mobility. We were products of the controversy of the slaveholding president, and we were divided, thus, conquered. Thomas Jefferson was the great philosopher and architect of colonial America based in Charlottesville, Virginia, in the state which has yielded the most presidents in American history: eight, and four of the first five. There was George Washington, Thomas Jefferson, and James Madison. There was James Monroe, William Henry Harrison, and John Tyler. And there was Zachary Taylor and Woodrow Wilson. A slaveholding state produced the most presidents in the United States' history. The federal feng shui started from Virginia plantations and mansions.

In the Charlottesville community, the black students were either exceptional or excluded: exceptional as in particularly talented in something and black at the same time, or excluded from the brainstorm of what the newly evolving American dream was going to be. Only some of us black students were invited to think critically about the state of the world and science and language. All of us came from this lineage and this radius that was Monticello and the University of Virginia and the surrounding community with all of its theory and hypocrisy, and we were cautiously rationed civility. Being recognized and commended as black and intelligent was a beckoning into the aristocracy that lived in the public school system. And we dog paddled through passive aggression in the school hallways past the sanctum of the libraries. It was an aristocracy composed mainly of area whites who lived in the nice neighborhoods and whose parents had the dream jobs in law, medicine, government, architecture, and real estate. There were a few successful black families with kids in the school system, but not many. From the vantage point of the ghetto experience, people like me peeked at White America.

During my first semester at the University of Virginia, of particular note and gossip then was the affair that Thomas Jefferson had had with Sally Hemings, one of his slaves. I remember this being news around campus that black students found a fountain of a hot topic around which we meekly convened and speculated. This obviously was scandalous, but also obviously meant humans had some things in common, like we are all the same color when the lights go out. And maybe even God bless the mulattoes who softened hearts and tugged at the consciences of lawmakers. We shared a past, and we shared genealogy, and we also shared disdain for each other, and by this point in history, we had already known that there really was space enough for everyone and we didn't even need to be segregated. As a child, I circulated through this area, unaware of that sort of master-slave relationship. What I knew was that slaves did the work, and the master told them what to do. If they didn't do the work, then they were whipped. We also heard the occasional story, however vaguely conceivable, of the slave buying his or her freedom. Having to buy one's freedom could not have been such a simple thing in and of itself, but it was taught to be the alternative to escape. It was true, but why would you believe that if you had never seen it?

Teachers and textbooks presented slavery as being an isolated relationship of cause and effect, with the description of psychological ramifications of black versus white being rebellion and escape, or the captive learning to love the captor, which we have learned to call Stockholm Syndrome. Is what we as black people do now a syndrome, or is it really a survival skill? Does the American school system really give us the skills to survive as the collared black psychology versus the infrastructure of white policing is the story? Being that young, I never pondered the actual sophistication of the power that the master had over the slave through federal legislation and intimidation. We didn't know that then. I never had that lien on white psychology and all the bonfire of their vanity. Did my Big Brothers know about all that? Sure they did. Were they aware of how audacious our relationship would have been back then? Sure they were. When I went off to places with my white Big Brothers, I bet my mother saw those instances through the filter of the once-upon-a-time precedent of Dred Scott vs. Sanford.

You can see that same leverage in marketing schemes and politics today. You can see the divide of a system that has been able to legally segregate your parents but not you. Linguistically and psychologically, the master had an awesome advantage as the slave had to wait around for his humanity to be realized. That's why black people still expect to be compensated for it. And that's why we as black people have such a hard time with self-discipline now, because of what discipline was back then. There is relatively little inclination in the black community to learn new languages and talk about mental health, yet we all know that we want to escape the brainwashing.

    I saw my parents answer to white people who were their bosses all the time, like "good slaves" so to speak, and that was white people disciplining my black parents. One day I saw my dad have trouble explaining why he had missed a shift at Greek's Restaurant and Grill in Blacksburg, Virginia, where the five thousand dollars a week he made there was what he described as 'good money'. It seemed that my dad was telling a lie whilst explaining and that he was slightly uncomfortable doing it, and even more uncomfortable making up that story while I was there. That was the psychology of discipline apart from the parenting they provided me. This was small business and corporate hierarchy, and this was what happened outside of the house during the day in the working world. When we saw how white people were the boss, it was something we weren't supposed to have seen. It was the collective lump in the black throat. Only rarely was a black mom or dad an H.N.I.C. In fact, Beverly Cleary and Judy Blume showed us what adolescence was going to be. These authors first showed us what the internalized voice of puberty was just a little bit before we would actually start the process. However controversial these painted ladies were in real life, we saw that sense of rank in white and black relationships around town, and we also read about their white family dynamic as the preferred narrative for the development of emotional intelligence. We rarely read about black adolescent characters and what they were feeling. But we did have Levar Burton on Reading Rainbow being our spokesperson for the joy and rewards of reading. He was a part of the good foot forward for black identity.

    My mom had been muscling me and my younger brother,

Marquis up from the ghetto to middle America year by year, mostly by herself, as I took to the immediate rhythm of poetry; I guess because I didn't know how to connect anything more. My thoughts came in spurts, and structuring them into some type of narrative or scholarly writing was neither my strong point nor my inclination, so I reckoned to hold fast to poetry and my dream of being a famous poet, and I wouldn't escape my box until later in life. I was affecting the perception of my community in a good way because I had seen what upward mobility was because of my mother, but I always doubted my individual effectiveness. The outlet that supposedly gave you power, the pen, and the usual place people who looked like me ended up, the penitentiary, remained a double-entendre.

After getting accepted into Kenyon College, Oberlin College, Middlebury College, and the University of Virginia, I stayed home for college and went to school at UVA. I also audaciously applied to Princeton and Duke, but I wasn't accepted. UVA was familiar to me. I had been a Little Sibling. I was a student at the UVA Summer Enrichment Program for several summers and the Young Writers Workshop at the Curry School of Education a few times. The Summer Enrichment Program wanted us students to explore and develop our own interests, think critically and creatively outside the box, and produce our own authentic scholarship and art. At the Young Writers Workshops, we could choose between fiction, poetry, and playwriting. I chose poetry because I was a poet and I knew it. In addition to my involvement in camps and workshops, and by the time I was ready to apply to universities, my family also had had a legacy situation at the University of Virginia because my aunt and my cousin had studied at UVA, too.

I am one of Charlottesville's own, and I remember very well

being nine years old and wanting to be a part of things at the university in my hometown. It was the late eighties, and environmental awareness was on the rise, and the internet was developmental. My Coltranian giant steps and adult strides today easily surround and interrogate my little adolescent feet and tiptoes from back then. Every testimony to the black experience at the University of Virginia is pivotal as we are all presumably trying to experience a better life with some sense of purpose. I think it's safe to presume that. Every black person that has been accepted into the University of Virginia, or any of its subsidiary programs, has a particular story to tell and constitutes that mosaic. It is a very peculiar institution, in a very peculiar geographic location beneath the watchful and lazy lion gaze of Monticello and UNESCO, where money and name recognition do the talking.

Medusa

The University of Virginia is well known for its Greek life with its fraternities and sororities. Several fraternity houses in the same neoclassical style of architecture peer from the edge of Madison Bowl on Rugby Road. I would say that about a third of the students at UVA belong to a fraternity or a sorority and explore the tenets of like-mindedness. Mark and Bill were both in the SPE fraternity, or Sigma Phi Epsilon. Kip wasn't in a fraternity. Thomas Jefferson's neoclassical designs house some of UVA's finest, and they pulse through the circulatory and lymphatic systems of the Academical Village.

Fraternities and sororities focus on scholarship, leadership, and community service. They also love to party. They emphasize brotherhood and sisterhood in their academic pursuits among the student body and in the surrounding community. Mentoring and tutoring in disadvantaged communities and climate change are arguably the two main spheres in which students volunteer. Joining the corpus of a frat or sorority can mean lifelong friendships and valuable networking for later on in life. UVA's fraternities and sororities spend a lot of time contributing to the Charlottesville area through volunteering, mainly through the Madison House programs. Students govern individual fraternities and sororities, and the governing council of all the collective fraternities and sororities at UVA is student-led. UVA is home to sixty-two chapters of fraternities and sororities, and also the Inter-Sorority Council, the Inter-Fraternity Council, the

National Pan-Hellenic Council, and the Multicultural Greek Council.

In Greek mythology, Medusa was one of the three Gorgons who reluctantly turned people who looked at her into stone. It became a challenge for the area warriors and explorers to kill her, but all of them failed, becoming statues in their attempts because they looked at her. Medusa had been cursed, but Perseus managed to behead her by using a bronze shield he received from her goddess, Athena. By using the shield as a mirror, he didn't technically catch eyes with her. He then used her head like a lantern, which still had the power of petrification even when not attached to her body, against other foes on the return route home from his quest.

Medusa is a unique figure in Greek mythology and was the only mortal of her siblings. She was not always the notorious Medusa with snakes as hair that everyone knows about. In fact, if you look at the phonetics of the name Medusa from a Slavic perspective, "Med" translates to "honey" and "dusa" translates to "soul". She was originally attractive and alluring, with glorious hair. She was, however, rumored to be very boastful of her beauty. She was cursed by Athena because of a forced affair she had with Poseidon, the god of the sea. Unsympathetic Athena was also beautiful, but she was jealous because Medusa's beauty rivaled hers, and everyone knew it. Poseidon made repeated advances at Medusa because he was infatuated with her, but she was not interested. Poseidon had also had his differences with Athena and saw that winning Medusa's heart would also have been revenge against Athena. However, Medusa did not want Poseidon because she knew she must remain a virgin as she was one of Athena's priestesses.

Athena did not help Medusa as Poseidon raped her and got

her pregnant on the steps of Athena's temple. Maritime Poseidon vanished after raping and impregnating her, and his act made Medusa his wife by default. Athena punished Medusa instead of Poseidon because punishing the gods was unthinkable. Men who gazed upon Medusa's eyes would turn to stone instantly. She had no chance for any encounters with men she potentially liked because she would turn them to stone as well.

Athena accused Medusa of betrayal and turned the hair that she envied into snakes and banished Medusa from civilization. Athena effectively canceled Medusa – like you see victims of cancel culture on the internet today. Medusa was also afraid of herself as she struck a petrifying fear into onlookers. Her anger at the gods was legendary, and so was her reputation, as she had been relegated and exiled under horrible circumstances. Perseus was Zeus's son and the one who would ultimately carry out Medusa's demise and put her out of her misery. He did it to save his mother Danaë, who was being forced into marriage with King Polydectes of Seriphos.

There had been a prophecy that Perseus would kill his mother's father, Acrisius. Acrisius, trying to prevent the prophecy from coming to pass, had locked Danaë in a castle to keep her from having a child. Zeus heard about Acrisius locking Danaë in this castle and intervened by transforming himself into golden rain that impregnated her with Perseus. After Perseus was born, Acrisius tried to further prevent the prophecy from happening by locking Perseus and Danaë in a chest and throwing them into the sea. The chest wound up washing ashore on the island of Seriphos, where Polydectes was king. The king's brother rescued them. After some time, Polydectes would meet and fall in love with Danaë, but Perseus did not like him. Perseus had become a grown man, but a poor one, yet very protective of his mother and would not let King Polydectes near her. Polydectes needed to get Perseus out of the way long enough to force Danaë into marrying him. So, he proceeded to act as if he was going to marry another woman, Hippodamia, and invited the people of Seriphos on the condition that they bring a gift. Perseus could not attend because he had nothing, but he promised to get Polydectes whatever else he wished. Polydectes sent him on the historically futile mission to fetch the head of Medusa. This way, Perseus could never prevent the marriage between him and Danaë.

With such high stakes, Perseus would need help from the gods and got it: Hades gave him a helmet that made him invisible to Medusa and her sisters; Hermes gave him a pair of winged sandals that allowed him to fly to Medusa; Athena gave him a bronze shield that was able to reflect Medusa's petrifying gaze; lastly, he was given a sword by his father Zeus that was sharp enough to cut off Medusa's head. Perseus succeeded because he was able to look at her reflection with the mirrored bronze shield. He could see her when she made her move to strike and kill him. He successfully countered her attack and killed her instead. After beheading Medusa, her two unborn children, Pegasus and Chrysaor, exited the wound in her neck.

He kept her head in a bag as it would help him later defeat Atlas, who tried attacking him on his way back to Seriphos. He then used it to turn King Polydectes to stone so his mother would not be forced into marriage with him. The blood leaking from Medusa's head was said to combine with seaweed to form the coral of the Red Sea as Perseus rested in Ethiopia, where he would also rescue and marry Andromeda. Perseus ultimately gave Medusa's head to Athena, who then placed it on her shield in what is a very sad and perplexing end to her story.

My mother and father's story began when they met on Dice

St. through my mother's cousin, right above where my uncle Clarence lived. I had a rather velveteen rabbit childhood without both parents under the same roof. I spent a lot of time wondering what it would be like to have my dad living in the same house. Legend has it that my uncle Clarence once hit my dad across the face with a cold, wet, and solid (as my father put it) ax handle. Uncle Clarence was one of nine brothers, all of whom were very protective of my mother and aunt. My aunt Esther is the youngest of my grandparents' children and my mother's only sister.

When I angle the looking glass and look back, I remember I was standing outside of my uncle Clarence's house, talking with him as he sat. I had found out from somewhere how some people have a photographic memory. I remember being dejected when I figured that I was not one of these gifted people, and I told him that I wished I had one. He looked at me and laughed and sighed at the same time, and he reassured me that I did have a photographic memory because I always remembered him whenever I saw him.

I have never wanted to learn to play dice, even though it is such fodder for black folks. All the gangsters shoot craps and play cee-lo. I used to see us winning and losing money with it. I always saw the men blowing inside their balled-up fists like it was cold outside and subsequently interjecting a James Brown-like "heh" when the two or three dice had finished tumbling from their hand to the ground and came to their separate standstills, staring back at the group with a solitary number on each one. The people around you knew your fate just as soon as you did.

Uncle Clarence has since passed away from cancer, as have three other uncles – two from cancer and one from a heart attack. My mother's father passed away from cancer, as well. Cancer is common in my family, but I just try to eat well and exercise enough so that I don't really worry about it. My father has always been a chef, and my mother has primarily worked in healthcare or in the care of people and assisted living. She also used to work for a legal publishing company. All my terrestrial sense and discipline comes from my mother, who has never done drugs or alcohol and has always been a very grounded person. My extra-sensory side comes from my father, who used to smoke a lot of marijuana, even while I was around. I remember the day he showed me what a "dime" was. Years later, I figured out that I could get high and enjoy it, and that's what I started doing, just like my father. Both my terrestrial sense, or common sense, and my extra-sensory side make me who I am. Through it all, work has a rhythm, people are wrong a lot; and they don't have to be right about you, especially if you never defend yourself.

As Greek mythology promotes white heroism and privilege, the Bible and its geography offer evidence to the contrary, not that each race doesn't deserve its own heroes. My Christian upbringing and the scriptures have helped me through a lot of pivotal times and explain how the world works, given people's personalities and world history. I really believed the prophecies of success placed on my life when I was younger. And I accepted that energy from those older church members who placed their hands on my peanut head while they prayed with olive oil and told me those things about how I was a child of God and how there was something special for me out in the world. And I didn't believe in spite of anything. It was an organic and maybe naive belief at the time, but the nature of our Christian faith made it substantive.

Growing up in a Christian household and family was a challenge of humility and vigilance. It seemed like hell as we watched our parents recover and preserve their humanity. It was real irrigation as we went to church twice a week to cultivate our faith. We went to Bible study once a week, and we went to regular church service once a week. We were never part of any rich congregation, and I often watched my mother struggle to pay her tithes. Nobody waited for my family to be charitable, and no organizations ever expected any hefty contributions. We sang worship songs, prayed together, and studied Bible teachings. We fellowshipped with black and white families in the area. We saw the spirit move in our own fellowshipping, and we saw it as visitors in other churches. Our week revolved around the promise of Mount Zion and not Mount Olympus. I did not grow up in my father's house, the man to whom I attached a god-like status, and I resent that incomplete relationship that constitutes the disorientation I felt growing up. Your own dad not in the house is a critical absence. Young men's sense of self-care, hygiene, dealing with adversity, making the most of opportunities, and chivalry should hinge on the fact that you have the guy who should have been your original everyday role model there. Dads are supposed to inspire gallantry. But as much as every man enjoys his own little sense of his own mystery, despite responsibilities he may have unintentionally created for himself, it can be easy to abandon your circumstances. It can seem like relief.

Hundreds of times I heard, "Boy, you look just like yo' daddy!" Everyone in town knew my dad used to work at The Boar's Head Inn Country Club in Charlottesville. If I had a dollar for every time I heard how I looked just like my father when I was growing up, I would be rich already if I invested it right. He is almost exactly twenty-three years older than I am. My mom and grandmother both have the same birthday, so that would have been cool if I had had the same birthday as my father. I am among the first males to finish college from my father's side of the family; maybe I was the first, unless my cousin Rodney or uncle Michael finished and beat me to the spiked punch. I figured this out somehow a few months before completing my last couple of classes for my degree in French Language and Literature from the University of Virginia. I studied in college what I loved to do in high school, and that was French. It was the language of love, and I had an ear for it. Learning French was very easy for me, and it was a new skin. I was the best around at it. It really boosted my self-esteem growing up. I was always so confident in my French classes in high school. I always expected an A on every assignment, and I was devastated when I saw otherwise. I knew that I was going to major in it in college and eventually move to France and live there one day. I even won a Jefferson Cup as the best foreign language student in my senior class in high school. Looking into Edgar Allan Poe's small preserved dorm room for a giant poet on the West Range at the University of Virginia upkept by the Raven Society, I can see myself in there, surrounded by those spartan essentials of a desk, a bed, a chair with books and a plume, and an oil lamp in unlucky number thirteen on the West Range just across the street from Alderman Library.

Inner Sanctum

When I was in elementary school, I loved to show all my classmates and teachers how I could read and how quickly I could do times tables, and I was always surprised when someone would lie contrary to my truth I was telling about them or about something they had done. I knew that I was a gifted student, yet that I was not from a nice white neighborhood like a lot of my friends and most of my teachers. I noticed black versus white first, and Asians, but I was certainly aware of the other demographics. We all knew who the deaf and blind students were. People in wheelchairs were conspicuous. You could tell which students' families didn't have much money. You could tell which students did not bathe regularly. Those were the most immediately visible things, but I had all kinds of friends, and I tried to fit in with everyone.

Headline news went in one ear and out the other through my head, and I always halfway listened, pretty statically, to things that were going on in the news in the United States and around the world. Nightly news anchors docked at the port of our television, and when things happened, I just sat still and watched how grown people at school and in my family reacted. Things like the Cold War, the AIDS epidemic, when the Challenger exploded, Tiananmen Square, Jeffrey Dahmer, the dissolution of the Soviet Union, Saddam Hussein and the Gulf War, David Koresh and the Branch Davidians, etc., were very real things that seemed to hit home with the rest of society, but not with me. I was generally in my own world and meditation the whole day, anticipating the next lesson and my next teacher's set of quirky characteristics. Most of them were fascinating adults with nerve, who frankly made us aware of behaviors they would not tolerate. A few of them were pushovers who routinely acquiesced, which let us know things we could get away with.

Outside the hub of the school day, until about nine or ten years old, my life was in and around various housing projects. Three things about my childhood that come to mind are my green drinking cup, a distaste for radishes, which were too hot, crunchy, and bitter for me, and hiding food that I did not want underneath the refrigerator. I usually hid food that wasn't sweet up under there as other regular food caused me routine nausea. I loved to eat syrup sandwiches on wheat bread and pour sugar into condensed milk until it became pink and sweet. I was the youngest of my mother's children until I was six. I was third. My cousins and other neighborhood girls were my babysitters-by-committee back then while my mom was at work.

I loved the playgrounds in the neighborhoods we lived in, and I loved shortcuts. There is something stabilizing about knowing where shortcuts are. It's comfortable knowing that they are in your neighborhood between and behind buildings, and down hills connecting to highways and other familiar houses in surrounding neighborhoods. They can leak in and out of playgrounds. They can be an easy exit and a triumphant point of entry after ascending a steep hill overgrown with grass, weed, and briar from the outside world of neighborhood periphery. The playgrounds were places where I could go and have quiet time with myself, and I did not have to venture too far off. I loved to play in the sandbox, and I loved to use the merry-go-round. But life then was a negative experience from which one would have to work very hard to overcome. For a few years, I was an only child trying to keep up with my single mother. But playgrounds were a fair escape. Most people living in housing projects stayed there, but not us. We would eventually find stability through a very laborious and itinerant upward mobility. I don't know how much my existence motivated my mother, but I like to think I was the rationale for her wanting to improve her lot in life as a single woman. She had already been married and a young divorcée. After Marquis was born, I guess her sense of urgency heightened, and good things started happening more quickly. Soon, we were in a regular house with a yard, and no longer in housing projects.

 I remember getting picked up from Clark Elementary School in her green Maverick. I can't believe that I was ever that small of a person keeping a cycloptic eye on a grown woman. I remember certain days in Ms. Utz's kindergarten class, and I remember some lunchtimes and filing out of the cafeteria single file with other kids in Clark school. I remember lying and peeking during nap times at the prizes that we would get after waking up. I always peeked at the prizes that Ms. Utz would lay on the floor, but never directly at her, of course. I lay there and looked through the prison bars of my fingers that covered my face. We always played "duck, duck, goose" in Ms. Utz's class, and that was how we could tell which girls liked us. Whoever liked you would tap you as they walked by, especially if they walked by once to calm their nerves a little bit and then tapped you. I also remember sitting and surmising at the summit of the steep steps in front of the school and waiting for the familiar and bold entrance of that olive green Maverick, and also the raspy hum of her Maverick's successor aqua green Honda Accord. The Honda was an upgrade from the Maverick, and she was really proud of it when she got it. I followed her lead and knew to be proud of it, too.

Clark Elementary school, in the heart of the Belmont neighborhood in Charlottesville, Virginia, was my first of two elementary schools. After a year of kindergarten in Clark Elementary school, I started going to Jackson-Via Elementary school, where I would be through my fourth-grade year. Jackson is my mother's maiden name. When I was about to leave Jackson-Via, I began to get a reputation for being a gifted student, part of a smaller group of students who everyone knew were smart. We were the Jackson-Via Jackrabbits. We were the tortoise's nemesis in the Tortoise and the Hare fable. You can still find us on the many prairies, steppes, and plateaus all over North America. I made the White Man's Burden a relatively painless process when it came to teaching me things: I was pretty good at most subjects, but mainly math, science, and reading, and I wasn't at all rebellious, and I always paid attention. The students at Jackson-Via were a very diverse bunch. Neighborhoods were pretty mixed in that part of town. Jackson-Via was on Harris Rd., and Harris happened to be my grandmother's married name because of her husband, Roy. Almost directly across from the school was Welk Place, and to the left of the school was Longwood Drive. Both of these neighborhoods were on cul-de-sacs. My friend Rhonda, who looked white and had long and coarse red hair, always waited for her black grandfather to come and get her to walk her home from school.

I remember the hallways during Black History Month. These were the same hallways we always had to wait for the white kids to get checked for lice. All the black kids knew we couldn't get them. And I remember the library where Ms. Burton taught us what "gyros" were after the school lunch menu sent the student body into a querying frenzy over what was for lunch that day according to this completely new and perfectly foreign word. It was only obviously food to our local pairs of eyes because it was on the lunch menu. I had never heard the term "gyro" before. It turned out that Ms. Burton actually pronounced it wrong, as in with a hard "g" and a long "I" like the word "gyrate" or "gyroscope", and not like the word "euro", my father told me later. I learned that gyros were as popular to Greek people as tacos were to Mexicans.

On a regular basis, I received merit awards for proficiency in reading, math, and science, and I was known as an all-around intelligent little guy. But I loved to get perfect attendance awards the most, but that didn't happen quite as often as I wanted. I remember one night at dinner at my uncle William's house, my aunt was telling us about a kid who had perfect attendance all the way through school, and I just couldn't believe it! In first grade, I remember excelling in group reading exercises in Mrs. Akers' class, who coincidentally would end up teaching my niece some thirty years later in the very same Jackson-Via that I attended, even in the same classroom.

In second grade, I remember I was picked to be a kind of guide for a new international student from Afghanistan, whose family had fled the then Soviet War, in Ms. Dunsmore's class. She pulled me to the side one day after Hamid was introduced to us and confided in me the duties of showing Hamid the ropes of second grade. I felt important. I felt like an ambassador. Hamid and I became very good friends during that year, and I even visited his house and family. I now find myself having lived in Central Asia in Kazakhstan and Kyrgyzstan, learning Russian, giving that memory of Hamid an added significance. But after that school year was over, Hamid skipped a grade, and I lost my friend.

In third grade math, I could recite the answers to times tables the fastest in Mr. Jarrell's math class. I was Mr. Jarrell's prize student because of this. I am almost positive Mr. Jarrell was gay, without ever seeing him do anything gay. He never left the school with other men, nor did any other men ever come and visit him there. He just looked gay while doing things, not that I have anything against gay people. He was just the first of my teachers who I noticed was different. My mom always described gay men as "funny". She would say things about certain men like, "I think he's funny." or "He seems funny." I also would come to learn that I had a gay uncle in Germany who moved there to pursue music. Being gay was much more of a taboo thing back then, and there was much chagrin associated with the LGBT community. I knew I wasn't gay. Mr. Jarrell's class was also where I first learned about German, as we had had a new bilingual student from Germany enter our class midway through the school year. Toni was a hotshot who already knew how to write in cursive, and I remember being jealous of her because Mr. Jarrell let her write freely in cursive, but not the rest of the class. There was also a girl from Okinawa, Japan, who I just loved. Her name was Jennifer. These were two of the many girls on whom I had crushes.

In fourth grade, science predominated. My first black teacher had been my third grade science teacher from the year before, Mr. McGruder, whose son also went to the school. We heard about him, but I never met him until a few years later. Mr. McGruder let us cook up sugar crystals in science class, and everybody thought it was cool that a teacher had a son at the same school. Mrs. Harding had us doing hands-on things like hatching chicks in incubators, a step up in complexity from tending to third-grade sugar crystals. Mrs. Harding alleged that the state of

Virginia gave her the right to use a paddle, in loco parentis, as a disciplinary measure if students' behavior warranted such. That was my first memory of Mrs. Harding as a nine-year-old as I thought to myself, she better not hit me with that thing. I still loved Mrs. Harding and all of my science teachers. Her philosophy probably fostered many alliances and buddy systems over the years between her students, and I was so excited after hearing about the Big Siblings program. I rested assured concerning my soon-to-be new Big Brother in spe, as in SPE or Sigma Phi Epsilon.

    I knew it would be cool to have my very own Big Brother, like a pet with his own human. I also knew my mother would let me participate without any argument. I went home and told her about it, and after very little deliberation, she said it would be okay. Every day before I got the call about getting my Big Brother, I would peek in her room before she got home from work, being nosey and ready with anticipation to see the green, blinking light on her answering machine. I was preoccupied for weeks about the verdict to my inquiry and request. That blinking light on her answering machine, the machine on which she had carefully engraved her message about not being home at the moment in her white woman voice, would be the blinking light of the message from my new Big Brother, I postulated. My life was taking a turn. She called me into her room, after she arrived home from work and got herself together, to let me listen to the message. It was from my school guidance counselor, and it was what I had hoped. I was just a little premature about it actually being the guy. Ms. Gardner was the school guidance counselor, a lady who I didn't see that much, but she knew who I was. Ms. Gardner was pretty apparitional in those days, like a nice witch who signified good news when you saw her. I didn't see her that often, but when I did, I just knew things were all good. She walked around Jackson-Via just doing her job, and everyone knew the universe was in order when we saw Ms. Gardner.

Toward the end of the summer, I got a call from my actual Big Brother. I don't really remember what I said to him. I was just so happy about the opportunity to go out and do new stuff. This was the dude that was going to bring a new intensity and sensibility into my life. My mom had been laying the foundations of chores, discipline, and encouragement, but this was going to be a new phase of my life. Having good role models improves your relationships with other people. If you revere good role models in your life, it gives older people a reason to believe you are not completely going down the wrong path in life. It also gives friends in your age group something to talk about. My friends would always want to go along when I went to places with my Big Brothers. It started a healthy buzz in my family and among my teachers. Good-humored, articulate, and open role models encourage communication. Madison House is a nonprofit organization that provides mentorship for at-risk youth in the Charlottesville area. An at-risk youth is less likely to make a successful transition into adulthood from adolescence because of some disadvantage they incur in their upbringing or some noteworthy talent they have that can attract adversity or exploitation or be too much to manage.

Some students have a talent that is first-generational that no one in their family knows how to harness or shepherd. And just like it may really take someone from outside of the family to see talent objectively, it may take a third party to get through to a student who has been soured by experiences at home. These students' disdain or apathy for their communities and schoolwork is visible and intimidating at times. It's the elephant in the room.

Disadvantages a child experiences can be immediate and visible, and sometimes the evidence of some void will happen later in life, having been hidden during childhood. At-risk youth generally come from low-income families. Most have experienced some life-changing circumstances at an early age, such as the absence or death of a parent, sexual abuse, bullying or emotional abuse, or maybe have seen the effects of addiction. Sometimes their talent is extraordinary, or it may be some clever knack for problem solving that a teacher notices.

Sometimes gifted students are brilliant but troubled writers, talented yet distracted athletes, or introverts who enjoy the strategy of chess and enrichment from reading. Particularly gifted students are in more advanced classes, and there is no real significant history of this kind of scholarship in their families. They are twice part of a unique dichotomy of personalities in the spotlight. Everybody knows that something happened to them, but that it doesn't outweigh that special little certain something about them, but experts know how they typically fail.

So, the indications of being an at-risk child are good and sometimes not so good, as the definition of at-risk is particularly broad. But that which is mysterious to other kids is usually obvious to adults. A teacher or guidance counselor has already detected the at-risk kids, or it is plain as day on their student reports and makes them compelling enough to track. Kids with behavioral problems become an obvious time bomb, while the gifted students are ushered off into the advanced classes with the smart white kids and the Asians.

I don't mean to sound like a stereotyper, but the longer kids with behavioral problems have been in the school system, the more infamous they are. Students who visibly show their disdain are reluctant to participate, are very emotional, and are usually in classes where the learning and curriculum are not at a normal acceleration. They are always being sent to detention or being suspended and often develop into bullies and grow comfortably into their reputation as troublemakers.

Volunteers for these good and bad at-risk students are mostly white from more affluent backgrounds, and whether at-risk kids' households have told them to love or hate white people, the friendships you can find between the volunteers and the students can become genuine. Because learning and education can turn out to be nothing but pressure, failure, and anxiety for some of the students who don't understand the dynamic of it all, having a mentor helps. It can be a welcome relief, and mediation between family and schoolwork.

The possibility of escaping their negative situation either intrigues or discourages at-risk kids. To those whom it intrigues, reaching out to an organization like Madison House is natural. It just feels right to step through those gates and into that part of a new social life. The other sides of being human that you see in the different demographics that exist at public schools are out there somewhere, and here is a chance to find out what they are exactly. It's a chance to be bold and penetrating. It's a chance to represent your household.

Here lies that rite of passage and that sneak peek. Here is a chance to get out of the house for a few hours a week with a real college student and use cuss words and be corrupted, however much of a big secret it seems. Most kids with behavior problems are reluctant to involve themselves in that kind of freedom with someone from such a different world because it's too different and embarrassing, but they sometimes do step out on that limb and dare to open up.

It's a fair chance to show your stuff out in the real world. It's a chance to show your talent or how you really are outside of school hours. Your homeroom teacher announces the program during the school day early in the year. Everyone asks each other if they wanted a Big Brother or Big Sister and if they raised their hand when their teacher asked them.

People donate serious dollars to this kind of program because it means well. There are several other mentorship programs similar to Madison House Big Siblings across the country and around the world. Sometimes the dollars are not enough to cover expenses for high-volume areas where there are many disadvantaged kids. The program's mission statement is clear. It is a program that is here to help children who are at these financial or emotional disadvantages in life at an early age. What usually is the case is that where you find one of these disadvantages, you also find the other. The program wants to promote educational success and discourage risky and delinquent behavior by keeping kids out of the streets and engaged in constructive things.

Nonprofit organizations like Madison House are dedicated to furthering social causes. They are organizations that use revenue surpluses to strengthen the pursuit of their objectives and not as a purse for the administrators, shareholders, or board members. Nonprofits usually operate in religious, scientific, research, or educational contexts. One of the first jobs I remember my mother having was working for the nonprofit American Lung Association. Nonprofits are held accountable to donors, funders, volunteers, program recipients, and the area community. These organizations need public confidence because the more public confidence they have, the more donations they receive to carry out their missions. Religious organizations, educational institutions, and human service organizations receive the most charitable donations among all registered nonprofits in the United States.

There is definitely a glamorized side of the Charlottesville identity as a college town that drives the area high schoolers. The seed of college life is planted in every student's head at an early age, and it becomes a goal. My friends and I knew that if we did well in school, we would get into a good college and find a good job. As we got older, being popular became more and more of a priority. Boys got taller and more broad-shouldered, and girls grew into their hips, and breasts jumped out of their shirts. Best friends and tight-knit groups of friends were interrupted by boyfriends and girlfriends. Boy voices cracked up and into deeper and more authoritative tones. Girls began to let the boys take the lead.

The Neighborhoods I Lived in While Growing up in Charlottesville

Garrett Square

In all likelihood, this neighborhood I lived in was named after the famous Sheriff Pat Garrett, nemesis of Billy the Kid. Pat Garrett and my father share the same birthday: June 5th. Mark's nickname for me was "The Kid". Mark did not know I had ever lived in this neighborhood because we had just moved to nicer areas right before I was matched with him. To this day, I can still hear him calling me "kid" in my head.

My father and mother never got married, and I am the only child between them. Until I have my own wife and children, I am a dying breed; the only full-blooded Soubeyran and the last Mohican. Ugolin Soubeyran is one of the characters in the Marcel Pagnol book Manon des Sources. I was my mother's youngest child then for six years until Marquis was born. My father had been in a relationship with my cousin Vetta before my mother, which was pretty bizarre for me, in retrospect. Garrett Square is now and was Section Eight housing then, and still conspicuously stands out on Charlottesville's landscape to this day. It is obviously the ghetto, yet things are obviously improving around it.

I was an only child living with a single mom. I had my own room. My aunt and cousins lived in Garrett Square, too and they were my aforementioned babysitters. My mother had no car then, so this was convenient in that my babysitters were right across the parking lot. I had to wait for a few minutes for one of my cousins, usually Shang, to come and get me from our apartment for the day as my mother had to get to work. She was a receptionist for a team of pediatricians then. I remember her being a pedestrian and walking out of Garrett Square in the mornings on her way to work to this pediatric hospital, specifically in this green two-piece skirt suit. This was one of the first things I thought odd as a child: her in a suit. It made her look like a praying mantis, very obvious on the sidewalk. It was that kind of green.

Garrett Square was the first and only place that I saw my mother get into a fight. I remember the day my mother got into a fight with Honey. I could see everything perfectly, and Honey walked up to my mother, and then words ensued. My mother was specifically trying to avoid a fight and any kind of physical contact with her. Honey was close to her and seemed to be sniffing her like a dog. My mother was wearing a gold blouse and a sienna skirt with her hand up like a celebrity trying to avoid camera flashes from the paparazzi. When Honey pushed my mother, I remember seeing one of her breasts pop out of her bra, and Honey eventually wrestled her to the ground. My mother let out what was a cross between a shriek and a deep wailing a few seconds after that. Honey had started to bite her fingers during the fight.

She showed me the bite marks on her fingers afterward. I saw her pink flesh, and it looked like a dog bit her. Honey's daughter was in many of my classes in school, and she had a crush on me, but she was bigger than me. This made their fight particularly perplexing for my young brain and a new dilemma for my developing psyche. Our families were from the ghetto, and we were no Montagues and Capulets. I had already been having trouble escaping her advances in school as she would sometimes look at me and halfway smile and say how she loved me in a creepy voice like she was trying to haunt me about it. I played it cool, though, and went about my day, honestly still uninterested. Honey also had a son who was older than me, but he died young many years ago in a car accident.

Our family stood out in the community because my mother was very pretty, and my uncle Ricky and aunt Theresa did street ministry in Garrett Square's community center. We called it "The Center". My aunt and uncle were under the tutelage of a white lady named Mrs. Brown. Her first name was Edna, and her husband was Douglas. I never heard anyone call them by their first names, except when Mrs. Brown called Mr. Brown Douglas. We saw Mr. Brown struggle with Alzheimer's disease before he passed away.

Everyone in the neighborhood knew who we were. We sang songs and listened to Bible teachings every week. We ate there and fellowshipped together with other families, friends, and community members. My aunt and uncle encouraged the community with messages that reminded them to be diligent and to praise God in all seasons of their lives. Mr. and Mrs. Brown lived on Azalea Drive, which was near Jackson-Via. The neighborhood is still called Azalea Gardens and is near the interstate exit out of the city of Charlottesville. You can get to Louisa County, where my mother was raised, by taking 64 East for about thirty minutes.

My mother had defected from her Hebrew-Pentecostal upbringing via this highway to what my aunt and uncle were teaching. My father was never there in my spiritual development. The doors were open for him to come, but he never ever came and made that kind of an entrance into that sphere of my life. My mother's mother was a Hebrew-Pentecostal who observed the Sabbath every Saturday in church. They celebrate Hanukkah instead of Christmas. The presiding elders of the church sit in the pulpit, while the other members sit in the pews where the speaker can see them from behind the lectern in the middle of the pulpit. The drummer and other musicians are to his or her right-hand side when looking out at the congregation from behind the lectern.

    Just like my father, my mother's father never really got into the church and religion during his adult life. While my grandmother was at church, everyone knew grandpa was at home working in the garden, feeding the dogs and chickens, or pushing the plough through the garden. Grandpa called all his grandkids "d.b." which was short for doll baby. My father's mother is a pastor; still, the only of her children involved in the church is my uncle Michael.

South First Street

After breaking up with my father, my mother dated a man who stabbed my father during a fight. We even lived with this guy in Baltimore at his mother's house for a while. This was the only man that I have ever walked in on my mother having sex with, like actually in the room. My father claims he died and came back to life after his run-in with Chet. He still has the scar on his belly, and it looks like a big worm. Chet, like in the word "hatchet" or "machete", was the man who stabbed my father.

My family also did street ministry in this housing project. We called its community center "The Center", too. The Center was ideally to be a humble little stem and axis of evangelism whose centripetal force, Mrs. Brown, was essentially a five-foot white lady teaching about the rose of Sharon and the lily of the valley, who was Jesus Christ. South First Street was really close to my father's apartment on Ridge Street. From The Center, we could see Lankford Avenue, which turned right and left onto Ridge Street. I remember seeing my father at the back door of our apartment on First Street one day, but I did not know why. In Garrett Square, the sofa was cut up one day, and I remember that my mother was complaining that Chet had done it.

Back then, my young mind could not really grasp how technical a correlation this was. It never registered to me as a betrayal, even years after my father told me the story, and I loved Chet all the same. I still automatically smile whenever I see Chet, which isn't so often now. It's been years since I last saw him.

That is a pretty significant thing because you would think a son would be vengeful against the man who stabbed his father in the gut. Chet was a tall, strikingly handsome, and light-skinned man. He looked like he was in the NBA. He always kept his hair cut short and low. He came, and he went. I knew that Chet was not my father, and he was relatively safe to be around from what I had actually seen of him. All the men my mother dated knew that I knew they were not my father.

Our apartment on South First Street across from the Ix building had a very thick gospel hearth. Ministry was working. My mother would play The Winans and Andrae Crouch records when she was cooking or cleaning. She played her gospel music from her single record player, very careful not to scratch the records with the needle. My oldest brother damaged several needles trying to scratch records like a hip-hop DJ.

I remember the personalities of my neighbors the most during our time on First Street. There was my best friend Derrick and his sister Veronica, "Ronnie-Boo", and their grandmother, who caught me and Veronica in the bed one day as she was enlightening me to exactly what it was that adults did in bedrooms, before I would actually see it with my own eyes. I remember Ronnie-Boo had a Big Sister with Madison House, too, about whom I often heard her bragging.

There was also Ralph, whose father was in a wheelchair. Every time I went into their house, I could feel how solemn the living room was with this handicapped man and schoolteacher, always sitting there in relatively low light. We always saw Ralph riding a grown man's ten-speed bike with one of his legs through the frame of the bike, beneath the top tube. His legs were too short to straddle the seat, but his resourcefulness was impressive. There was Gloria, who became Marquis's godmother, and our babysitter from time to time. There was also Ike, the winner in the first fight I remember losing, which was my first fight. And there was also Gladys, Jimmy, Lawrence, "Button", and Penny, the family that lived directly across from our apartment.

Derrick and I even started a fire on First Street. Billy Joel didn't. Derrick and I did. I remember it like it was yesterday. We had found a lighter, and we were lighting little scrap pieces of paper. Every piece we lit, we would look at for a while and then blow it out or stomp it out. Then one piece got a little too out of control as we sat still and charmed by the dance the fire did, and we did not manage to put it out in a timely manner. We both panicked and took off running, kinda sorta figuring we did not correctly extinguish it. I don't know what Derrick did, but I went and took a slightly nauseated nap at Gloria's house, thinking that I could go to sleep, wake up, and that little episode would be over. But hell was encroaching, and I awoke and knew something was up.

I peeked outside and saw a huge fire truck and then looked over at that patch of Derrick's yard we were in and saw a bunch of black burn markings on the grass like a car had sped off and left its tread marks. This was pretty major trouble I knew I was in if people found out we did this. This was the most trouble I had ever caused other than hiding my food under the refrigerator. I think I finally admitted it after acting like I had no idea what had happened. It took a few days, though. I honestly can't remember. Whenever Derrick and I got into an argument, I knew I could just sit outside on Gloria's porch with a little something to eat, and he would come over and apologize to get me to give him some of what I had.

Middleton Lane

"My yard is not a thoroughfare!" is what you heard from the kitchen window when my mother surveyed someone cutting through our backyard at 301 Middleton Lane. My mother was protective of her backyard in her new house that she was renting, and she did not care if you were black or white. L'enfer c'est les autres. My mother yelled at black people and white people from that kitchen window. This small brick house was the first house that we lived in. Just down the street from the once whites-only segregated Fry's Spring Beach Club was our house on the corner of Old Lynchburg Road, right before "Dead Man's Curve", which was a windy stretch of road with only an aluminum boundary separating drivers from a significantly steep drop into a sparsely wooded area.

My older brother Greg had the annoying habit of spitting on the floor of our room. I dreaded his visits. I already had to share the bed with Marquis, who was a whining pillow hog and a spoiled brat. Here we were in our new house, and he was just spitting on the floor whenever he felt like it. I sometimes felt his cold, gooey hog spit beneath my feet.

Jake, the mailman, saved Marquis from being hit by a car one day on Old Lynchburg Road. I never quite saw how he wandered into the intersection right before Dead Man's Curve; I just remember seeing him getting scooped up, immaculately preserved, and brought to safety by Jake. Marquis's father was, and still is, a cab driver. His relationship with his father was different from my relationship with mine. Marquis also had a Big Brother named Tony from Madison House, but Marquis never spent summers with his father. And Tony was black. He never went away for the summer like I did. Marquis's father was Charlie, and we did not know he was Marquis's father until he was in grade school. I had always thought that my younger brother's father was a man my mother had dated from Gordonsville, a small town in nearby Orange County (where you can find Montpelier and James Monroe's Highland plantation house). I thought this because we spent so much time in Gordonsville when I was young. We were always at Jimmy's house, where the one community highlight was the Tastee-Freez, which had good hamburgers, milkshakes, and other desserts. My mother dated Jimmy, and Marsha was Jimmy's sister. The toilet did not work in their house, and it was always filled with huge adult-sized turds.

 Middleton Lane was a steep hill that led up to Moseley Drive as you turned left from Old Lynchburg Road in Azalea Gardens. We also lived on nearby Camellia Drive, the first house we owned, in the same neighborhood during my high school and first couple of college years. My father was still living in Charlottesville in Ridge Lee Apartments on Ridge Street. His was the first apartment on the left as you entered the building, a mansion-esque kind of French-looking building with several rented suite spaces. He has four brothers: William, a.k.a. "Sunnyboy", Michael, Bobby, and Tibbs. I don't really know Tibbs that well, and I have only met him once. My uncle Bobby is a pool shark and looks like a white man. Uncle Bobby used to call me "headquarters" and also magically pull quarters out of my head through my ear and give them to me whenever he saw me at my uncle William's house.

I remember my visits to Ridge Street consisted of hanging out and eating, listening to music, and having conversations with my dad while we stood together on an imaginary ridge, overlooking the rest of the world and the universe. If I could have had my way then, I would have chosen to live with my dad full-time. This was just the partiality of a son's bond with his dad. Nothing else mattered when I was with my dad. I felt invincible, and I felt that we were invincible together.

I would listen to his Herbie Hancock tapes, Najee, Sade, and Tracy Chapman, among others. I love to listen to Sade songs and reminisce about summers at my dad's apartments in Blacksburg, just sitting in the living room. "Kiss of Life" is the song that I most closely associate with summers at my father's house. My dad used to wash my face with his spit, which I reluctantly endured for the five seconds that it lasted, especially on road trips for some reason. I would peek in my hero's corduroy notebook and other journal entries, where I saw evidence that this guy was actually human with feelings. I enjoyed rummaging through his things, peeping, pioneering, and commandeering through the mystery of his abode, finding all sorts of paraphernalia, e.g., roach clips, Sheikh condoms, seashells, etc. I loved the empty velvety Crown Royal bags he had hanging on his door knobs. He always saved his spare change for me when I came. I carefully rolled all the pennies he had saved before we would walk to the bank together and get the cash.

Whatever the source of problems was between him and my mother eventually found its resolution in events that followed their relationship. My mother went on to find peace and reconciliation through a second marriage, and my father got a chance to raise a son by raising my youngest brother, Josh.

Olinda Drive

My teenage years began on the cul-de-sac of Olinda Drive. Olinda Drive is where Mark and I had our first meeting. We always went to his fraternity house on Rugby Road to play hacky sack with some of his frat brothers. That tradition of hacky sack and juggling what was a hand-stitched rawhide equivalent of a scrotum in a circle of white guys in khaki shorts and old all-conditions gear sneakers was right about where I felt like being for some odd reason. These guys' lives orbited around the joy of completing a hack, which happened when everyone in the circle successfully touched the hacky sack without it touching the ground. Imagine the ebullient double hack or the euphoric triple. Once I had been deemed competent enough to complete hacks and extenuate to doubles and triples, I was accepted into the fold.

Mark had told me he used to play soccer when he was young. Upon hearing this, I was excited to follow in his footsteps, and I parlayed hacky sack into youth soccer. I started playing soccer when I was eleven. Part of being a young black soccer player back then was lauding the Brazilian National Team, mainly Romario and Bebeto, and Cafu for the defensive-minded. Then came the "Three R's" of Ronaldo, Ronaldinho, and Rivaldo. I loved Pelé and the Joga bonito history of Brazil. Joga bonito means "the Beautiful Game" in Portuguese where the Brazilian national team was known for playing with beauty, style and superb individual skills. Pelé was the best ever then, and there was no debate in my mind.

Mark showed me how to trap the ball with my chest, how to shoot, and how to chip the ball, among other skills, in his backyard in Connecticut. I remember the excruciating pain I went through trying to trap the ball with my chest, while he made it look so easy. It wasn't that he was good, it just didn't hurt his chest. It would take years before I was able to chest the ball without any pain. The ball we used was red and yellow, and cheap plastic. It had the same colors as the Kyrgyz flag. I would come to appreciate genuine leather, hand-stitched balls as I got older.

I was an above-average player that was very quick, but without breakaway speed, and not very strong. I was very small, but I had exceptional ball control, and thanks to Pelé and global media, I knew I could be the best one day. Although, I find it odd that Pelé was deemed a national treasure by the Brazilian government and was not allowed to play in the European leagues during the prime of his career. I find that to be unfair and confining. I was tricky with the ball, and I knew what I wanted to do with it. I always managed to dribble around Mark with ease. I would play with him and his frat brothers, and they always used to tell me that I was an exceptional player. I got a lot of confidence playing in those pick-up games with them.

I started to play rec league soccer and received the Future Star Award and team MVP honors in my first season. I still have the trophies in a drawer in my mother's living room. My coach Scott was also a Madison House Big Sibling, if I am not mistaken. We had the award banquet at a local pizza place, Anna's Pizza. Scott, and other youth sports coaches, had a similar "big brother" role in our lives. I was around future leaders, failures, and mediators. These were the years that I first started to accomplish outside of the school curriculum. I went on to play on the local travel team that played in competitions across the state. I started on the B squad and ended up on the A squad midway through the season. The B team was a little less talented than the A team. I had to prove I was good enough. We went on trips out of town to tournaments, and it felt good to be among the best players. In high school, I played for the junior varsity in ninth grade and the varsity team my tenth, eleventh, and twelfth grade years. I earned an honorable mention for the All-District team my junior year when I begrudgingly agreed to play fullback.

My best friend, Johnny, just so happened to live in the same house in the B apartment downstairs in the house on Olinda Dr., the basement house. My mom and aunts and uncles called my uncle Clarence Johnny, too. Just across the street from my house, there were some University of Virginia lacrosse players that were renting it, among them, the great Doug Knight – one of the best ever to play lacrosse at UVA.

Marquis and I always went to their house to get another perspective on college life. Marquis came up with the nickname "The Guys" for them. He would even go there on his own at six and seven years old, and everyone knew he was okay. He was just over at The Guys' house and would be back before it got too late. They would share pizza with us and let us have all of their old lacrosse equipment.

Next to them lived Sandra, who was secretly dating George and Greg's cousin Chris, and her racist brother Duane, whose custom was always to threaten to call the "lawman" on us every time we played too close to his monster truck in the street. Chris would make me call and ask for her as he dialed the number so no one would suspect it was him calling.

On the corner of Briarcliffe Avenue and Olinda Dr. lived Lucian Carter, the civics teacher at Buford Middle School – our black civics teacher. Just up at the top of the hill and to the right on Forest Ridge Rd. lived Shanika, one of my classmates, and her mother, Curlee, a local police officer. If you took a shortcut through the cul-de-sac onto Rockcreek Rd. you would be cutting through brother and sister Jermaine and Catrice's backyard. Another close friend of mine, André, lived on Rockcreek with his family, which included a stepfather and two brothers and a sister.

My neighborhood was interesting. Johnny, André, and I were always trying to get sex while my older brothers were experiencing it. The neighborhood was relatively safe and five minutes from Forest Hills park. My best friend was right downstairs from me. And it was a continuation of my mom's upward mobility because it still represented this step above where we had been accustomed to living. We were even the black family that lived in the main part of the house while the white family lived in the basement apartment. It should have been the opposite way around, according to what I had previously seen and known.

Mark had planned a few origami lessons for me from a man named Mr. Tanaka when we lived here. The whole event was kept under wraps until the moment it happened upon our instructor's arrival. I guess Sensei Tanaka lived in Charlottesville. Mark invited Sensei Tanaka to my house in my dining room at my dining room table with a leaf through the middle on Olinda Drive. He showed us how to make an origami tyrannosaurus rex, an origami crane, and an origami iris. He also showed us how to make several polyhedrons out of multiple sheets of paper: a dodecahedron from twelve sheets of paper; a cube, or hexahedron, made out of six sheets of paper; a tetrahedron, which uses three sheets of paper and looks like a type of pyramid; and, a little wallet out of two sheets of paper.

Thirty years later, I can still make that tyrannosaurus rex, that crane, and that iris and all those polyhedrons, among other things. I was sure to keep folding and folding until they were permanently in my head without having to refer to the directions. It was so cool to make all those neat little things from square pieces of paper. I have made a lot of good first impressions and started many pleasant conversations after making origami for people. I remember all my friends at school being amazed that I could make such things out of paper. I took it upon myself after those first couple of lessons to learn some other origami pieces. If anybody wanted me to teach them how, I would gladly sit with them for a few minutes and show them.

My brother, neighborhood friends, and I were latchkey kids. We were usually home alone until our parents got home from work. This gave us time to create all kinds of mischief for those couple of hours each weekday. We would do origami, sit and play video games, do the daily chores, answer any incoming phone calls, and generally just man the house and yard until everyone got home. Sometimes Johnny would come up to our house, or we would go down to his house. We would go to the park or somewhere close by, too. We figured out a lot of stuff back then in those few hours with no supervision. We played all kinds of sports outside in the street; we played soccer, lacrosse, football, badminton, and did skateboarding and rollerblading. Johnny was a special baseball player, and we always went up to Forest Hills Park near our house to play baseball. I always took a backseat to Johnny when it came to baseball, and I was always trying to help him get better by pitching to him like it was batting practice. It made sense because he was the only one of us who could hit home runs. I knew to defer to him because he was the savvy one on the baseball diamond. I was the origami guy.

For as much as I liked to play and explore during those few

hours each day, I always had chores to do, as well. If I didn't make sure to do the housework, especially wash the dishes and clean the kitchen, I knew I would get in trouble. It was automatic. It was a no-brainer. Cutting grass, raking leaves, and shoveling snow were seasonally a part of the chores as I wasn't ever one for manual labor back then, but I did it when I had to. We got yelled at when we let our responsibilities just sit there and pile up.

Camellia Drive

Camellia Drive was the house we lived in during my high school years. This was the primary scene of my mother's second marriage to James, who worked at UVA. This is the first house we owned. This is the house where I had my first computer, thanks to Mark. This is the house where I first experimented with alcohol and was an often reluctant accomplice to my older brother and stepbrother's shenanigans, which involved smoking tobacco and coming in the house at all hours of the night. Both of them knew that they could knock on my window, and I would get up and open the door whenever they decided to break the curfew.

Escaping what was becoming my mother's new household with her new husband became more and more of a priority. I certainly never expected anyone to take on that responsibility of freeing me from it because I knew I was in control. I did not need any help, and I did not need to be liberated. I knew I had a life outside of that house because of my experiences with Madison House. I was the oldest child living with my mom, and I knew how things worked there. I knew how my mother was. I had been the barometer. She had been my single mother before my little brother or James happened. There was always a dramatic tension associated with James. Brandon was James' son from his first marriage and really didn't have anything to do with me, and he and Greg were not always there living with us. There were just a couple of times when they lived with us.

I knew James had this nerve to come into my family life and assume that he was the boss of the house. We argued, rebelled, and I warned him about trying to be my father when he knew he really wasn't. I made it a point to make the distinction very clear, when opportunities presented themselves, to let this man know that he was not my father. To this day, he still insinuates that I should call him something other than his name. Back then, he was my mother's new husband, but he was not my father. We shouted and cried and often went to sleep angry. I was the one who held the strongest conviction about just how extended and just how nuclear my family was becoming. I was her child, all the while closely and circumspectly making sure this new guy didn't overstep his boundaries. It was tiring being that vigilant. It was distracting and worrisome. I, just like any child, was defending my mother's integrity against this guy who was always walking around like he was the shit. Sometimes he would just start cursing her out, and the first time he ever did came as a total shock to me. He was ornery and difficult to deal with. But I had to respect him because my mom had made this choice to be with him.

The house felt too patrolled by him as we became older. There was a quiet uneasiness about what discipline was and what it was becoming because of him. This was the particular difficulty in co-existing there. I felt like he was passive-aggressive and that he expected us to be in line just a little too much for someone who wasn't actually our father. His excuse was that he had been living a nightmarish reality of being a Vietnam veteran and recovering alcoholic at the same time.

Understanding this dynamic was critical to understanding how self-absorbed he was. Some people have a problem and assume you are just supposed to tolerate their resentment. There are some alcoholics who quietly go about their recovery, and there are others who make sure that you realize that maybe it's a blessing for you that they decided to recover. They have this tendency to remind you that you could very well be their next victim in some way, or that if things had been different, you may very well have been one. James was one of those people. Many of the males in my family are like that, and very passive-aggressive.

James had been a medic in the Vietnam War. As kids, we really couldn't ascertain or process that kind of thing, although we had seen wars on the news reports, and we knew that to die for your country was one of a few rare and noble things. To have been in Vietnam and to have had to come back to a country that despised you makes you some type of way. I suppose it turns you into something you most likely wouldn't have been under other normal circumstances. This facet of postwar psychology I figure I will never have to deal with, but it's also one I am not going to be victimized by. I can understand the conflict that it creates, but it's still no excuse to be abusive to people. This war in which he had been involved in French-occupied Vietnam gives my mother's and his relationship a depth, however. I suppose it's the stuff novels are made of, but you can't expect a child to understand that kind of thing, but as he or she grows older, things become clearer. That adult can look back at what happened as he or she is, hopefully, less egocentric, but maybe more callous against the past, yet understand the less obvious things at play. That's why I rarely visit the United States anymore because I am still angry at those circumstances.

At any rate, Camellia Drive was like a blast from the past for me. I had a new neighborhood best friend, who had been my friend at school since we were in elementary school. Arthur lived right over the hill on his lot on the other side of Camellia Drive. He, my cousin, Alex, and I always used to play together a few years earlier when I would come to Alex's house. So, I knew Camellia Drive and Azalea Park pretty well. But my uncle and aunt had recently moved to the North Berkshire neighborhood, so we were no longer a triumvirate. Arthur and I were pretty much inseparable when we lived on Camellia Drive. We were always into something. I usually got the better of Arthur in competitive things like basketball and football. I had a nickname for Arthur; I used to call him "White Boy Roy"; later, just plain old Roy. Roy's dad was named Artie, and his mother was Lula. Mrs. Drumheller has passed away, and I went to her funeral to pay my respects. Mrs. Drumheller loved me like I was her own, and my mom loved Arthur the same way. I was always having lunch or dinner at Arthur's house, and Arthur knew he was always welcome at Mrs. Copeland's. My friend Seth also lived over on Willard Drive. We played together on the first soccer team I was on a few years earlier.

The Calks lived next door to us. They were as Puritan as Puritans could be, but I don't really know to which religion they adhered. I think they were Mennonites or Amish. They actually wore bonnets and nothing but dresses. The daughters never cut their hair. They had horses in their backyard. Everyone knew that I had a crush on Reagan, the middle daughter. This was around the time I started attracting more women than usual because I was getting older. I went to prom from Camellia Drive; I brought my girlfriend home from UVA to Camellia Drive; I used to make out with Reagan on Camellia Drive. All those years of futility on Olinda Drive finally changed.

Mark was off in Taiwan, busy being an investment banker, and Bill and Kip had gone on to live their lives, as well. And this was where I kept corresponding with Mark via this new thing called the internet, a portmanteau of the words "interconnected" and "network". The internet was the new thing back then, and Mark shipped me a computer to use for my latter high school years and the beginnings of my college life. It was a Macintosh computer, and I could use its modem to connect to the internet, cybersex chat rooms, and porn sites. The smut was on! I had Mark and America Online to thank.

I had run into one of the jewels of White America who willingly and graciously corrupted me with all of pop culture's spoils, even from thousands of miles away in Taipei. I did also use my computer for academic things. I remember he didn't send me a printer, and I told him. Then, he sent me an inkjet printer so I could write my papers and print out presentations for school. I felt so blessed to have my new computer. I always Windexed the monitor and kept the keyboard free of dust.

Ablative of Manor

Mark called his house on Maury Avenue in Charlottesville "Château Blasé", and it was where I hung out often with Mark and his roommates. He moved to this house after moving out of the SPE house. Mark left an answering machine message to all "American poppycock" who called. He left the message in a Frenchman's voice, advising all said American poppycock to leave a message. These days that house on Maury Ave. is an off-campus apartment complex. I used to love to go and hang out, which consisted of watching television or playing on the computer. I loved being around Mark and his friends, and I always looked forward to our next meeting. On days when there was a football game at Scott Stadium, all of the roommates would open their driveway and yard for parking during the game. I remember they used to charge people seven dollars a piece to park.

The house was probably five or six bedrooms on two stories, with an eclectic group of roommates, so there was plenty for me to get into and always someone to probe about college life while I was there. Mark lived in the attic room. I enjoyed being around that collegiate conversation, and I enjoyed being one of the guys. College life was my destiny then, and their candid conversations seemed a natural progression from my mother's generally laissez-faire parenting. Part of my perception of what was cool as a pre-teen was shaped during my visits to Château Blasé.

Mark bestowed his former penny collection and stamp

collection to me, welcoming me into the heritage. I learned from Mark that the technical name for stamp collecting was "philately". I also learned that during the years of World War II, the United States made pennies from steel in order to have more copper for the war effort. I rolled the pennies my father collected for cash, but I kept these pennies for numismatics. Mark's girlfriend Annie made me bracelets out of embroidery floss, symbolically linking me to those memories and that time in my life.

Mark and I won the three-legged race at the Madison House Big and Little Sibling Olympics. I remember it very clearly, and all of the area kids were there with their Big Brothers and Big Sisters. All of Mad (short for Madison) Bowl was filled with people and snacks and Gatorade. Mad Bowl is a big field shaped like a bowl that is in front of all the fraternity houses on Rugby Road. Prizes were everywhere, too. I have gone back to Mad Bowl every now and then to play pick-up soccer games.

From the bottom of Mad Bowl, I could see the SPE house and all the other houses on Fraternity Row on Rugby Road. The day consisted of events that required speed, agility, precision, and balance – coincidentally, the same motor skills that disappeared once one had drunk too much alcohol. Mark and I won the three-legged race by such a large margin that we could have walked the last quarter of the race and still won. We didn't gloat, though, and hurried across the finish line. Winning the three-legged race was so gratifying because we dominated all of the other competition, and all the spoils went back to Château Blasé.

Hanging out in a neutral environment particularly lessened the blow of not having my father in my house as a child. My stepdad at home was too abrasive to not conclude that something else manipulative was going on inside of his head, so my exchanges with that primary male in my daily life were nothing like my surrogate relationship with Mark. I felt included when I was with Mark; I felt like I had a different sort of best friend who was not in my peer group. Somewhere deep down, I knew I was a citizen and that I was exceptional. Mark even introduced me to his academic advisor, "Tico" Braun, who was fluent in Spanish and a professor in the Latin American Studies Department. I was only ten years old then, so this was very important for me to know such a higher-up. I took our meeting very seriously. I remember talking to Tico about what I wanted to be when I grew up. Tico was an ally, and I was happy about that.

Mark also took me to see a book talk given by the famous Nigerian author Chinua Achebe at the University of Virginia. Mr. Achebe was giving a talk on his world-famous book Things Fall Apart. Mark made me read it before attending the talk. It was about Obi Okonkwo, a gifted warrior and wrestler, and the problems he had reconciling a failed relationship with his notoriously drunk and lazy father, Unoka, in the fictional village of Umoufia in Nigeria. There is also the story of Obi's semi-adoption of Ikemefuna of the neighboring Mbaino clan, who was given up to Umoufia as a sacrifice because of the murder of one of Umoufia's women. Later, the elders of Umoufia would order Ikemefuna to be killed. Obi rose to fame in his village by easily defeating the champion wrestler Amalinze the Cat, who was previously undefeated and was known for his back never touching the earth. That's why the village people called him "The Cat". Mark got a copy of Things Fall Apart autographed by Mr. Achebe and gave it to me. I remember when Mr. Achebe died a few years back, and I remembered my copy of Things Fall Apart. Here I am today, proof that they can and do fall apart, but all is not lost, necessarily, when they do. In his New York Times obituary, it says Mr. Achebe was a part of a generation of West African writers who were coming to the realization that Western literature was holding the continent captive.

Mark, Bill, and Kip were my mentors and encouraged me to strive academically, and neither to take learning for granted nor failing too seriously. Learning not to take failing too seriously was probably the most valuable lesson that I learned growing up. Mark was a drinker, just like my father, just like my uncles. I saw a different side of drinking and alcoholism during my involvement with UVA when I was younger. It was a more glamorized scene than drinking at home. The white kids had the money to drink but still drank the cheap stuff. I remember the keg parties and beer pong way back then, and when I got in and decided to go to UVA, these things were among the first things I looked for because they were familiar. I remember always feeling at home at fraternity parties that some of my white friends would invite me to. I was from the area and had done this kind of thing before, so I was a pro.

I buttressed my personality with the fact that I could coolly navigate between the black scene and the white scene at the university because that was the type of upbringing I had, and that was the me that I was going to be – this versatile spokesperson-for-intermingling me. I was that type of guy. I felt a duty to be an ambassador between black and white people. I knew somewhere that this was my calling because I had seen it all, so I thought – I mean, my father dated a white woman, and I was the only black student in many of my classes and extracurricular activities in high school. I was the National Honor Society president. I also was in the French Club and on the varsity soccer team. I was also a distance runner on the indoor and outdoor track teams. And I had known Mark et al. at Château Blasé because of my history with Madison House.

I was also as smart as all the Asians, and the first love of my life was a Chinese girl that I met at the very same University of Virginia, at the Summer Enrichment Program some five years before my first year. She would never like me again after that because I was so scared to kiss her or engage in any P.D.A. (Public Displays of Affection). I was always a standout at the Summer Enrichment Program in athletics and other activities we used to do with the camp counselors there. Some of my camp counselors there even knew Mark. Mark was from Fairfield, Connecticut, and grew up in a huge palatial home with eleven bathrooms or so. If you come from New England, then Virginia is pretty much the gateway to the Deep South of the United States. Mark's house in Connecticut was such a magnificently large place with so many rooms and computers and technology. I absolutely loved just sitting in the den or exercise room or outside on their veranda and just absorbing the cool of their yard or having snacks and bottled drinks like ginger ale from their always full cupboard. Mark's house was near Fairfield University – "good ol' F.U.", according to Mark. I met his mother Betty, father Larry, brothers Perry and Tony, and Perry's wife, Jill.

Mark's father was a businessman who rescued failing companies with his expertise. Failure and things falling apart were his business. The time I went to Fairfield, I learned that Mark's father had been involved in resurrecting the Fleer baseball card company. As a young, avid card collector then, I knew Fleer to be among the mid-tier baseball card companies, along with Donruss and Topps. Despite Topps' synonymy with the heritage of baseball, Upper Deck cards were worth the most. They were premium. You only got a stale stick of chewing gum with every pack of Topps. Everyone who was anyone in card collecting coveted the gloss of the Upper Deck Ken Griffey, Jr. rookie card. I was jealous of Johnny when I saw that he had picked a pack of Fleer baseball cards and found a Ken Griffey, Jr. rookie card inside. We used to steal packs of cards back then from the local card shop and were eventually caught one day. The store owners told us that we were no longer welcome there. I'll never forget that day and the look of disappointment on the fellow's face when he told us that we had to leave Southern Cards. Thankfully, he didn't call the police on us.

Mark's mother worked at the Ford Foundation. I'm not sure what she specifically did there, but I believe it was something pretty important, as in a part of the administration or board of directors. I think she was part of a board that entertained offers for grants and funding requests for community service projects, studies abroad, etc. Larry put broken things back together and Betty was a key part in an administrative assembly line. During the day, the house was empty because Larry and Betty were both at work in New York City. My first memory of Betty was her explaining to me the versatility of tofu, in that it generally tended to take on the taste of whatever it was surrounded in. I saw her eating it in a soup when the family took me out to dinner one night, and I asked her what on earth it was because it was very odd to see it floating and white at the top of her soup.

Perry was Mark's older brother and the oldest of the three. Perry was a Harvard man who was married to Jill. Both Perry and Jill had spent time somewhere in Africa, I think in Uganda, and both spoke Swahili. I was taken by this point of interest concerning these two. At Mark's request, they began a dialogue in Swahili right in front of my virgin-to-Swahili eyes and ears. Swahili tumbled from Perry's mouth, and Jill's Swahili came tumbling after. I hardly knew what to say as African languages were hardly as advertised in my school district as European ones were. I never expected to find a little African corner in their huge house in conservative New England. My conversations with Perry were very terse and informative with me very interested in Harvard and its distinction as one of the finest academic institutions in the country. The same Upper Deck gloss I coveted I also found present on Harvard prospectus manuals and other Ivy League paraphernalia scattered about. Here was a survivor of the Ivy League ideal that I had heard so many things about. I was right in the middle of all this legacy, yet I thought Harvard was unattainable with such lofty prerequisites for admission. Superlative Harvard expected valedictorians. I was fairly intelligent, but I was an underachiever. I was more of an ore that needed some more refining before I would ever be able to add anything integral to the American machine. I was not in all AP courses in high school; I was definitely at least in advanced courses and a couple of AP courses. I was not from a New York City suburb in Connecticut, hence rooted in any New England tradition. I came from Garrett Square and South First Street in Charlottesville, VA. These were the neighborhoods that had found their way into my psychology, and these were the blueprints of my understanding of living and grammar. My neighborhoods were not notoriously in the news like a Compton, California or East Los Angeles, or a Southside of Chicago, so the hero from the hood motif was pretty much out of my reach and saved for national media attention. Those guys from there usually wound up in the NBA, or either died trying or were in and out of jail. However, from the origin of colonialism I lived in Virginia, right on the outskirts of Thomas Jefferson's Monticello, generally cast in a positive light when it came to media coverage, yet this is where physical and psychological dehumanization in this country began. The contamination of the black psyche started where I lived, in and amongst all those black stones that the builders refused. And there in that mansion of a home in Fairfield, Connecticut, I was watching two white people, obviously in hippie love, speak Swahili to each other. This is where I also saw that white people could actually learn from black people.

Tony was the youngest of the three. I guess I encountered Tony once or twice, and that was it. What I knew of Tony was he wanted a motorcycle and was evidently hiding the fact that he really had one from his mother. I found this to be completely and perfectly scandalous. Here was the rebel of the brothers. The first striking thing about Tony that I remember was that he said, "You bitch!" in gest to his mother. I was through and completely shocked that he had called his mother a bitch. My mother would have slapped me had I said that to her. Tony and I were similar in that I was the youngest once, too. Soon after our visit to Connecticut, Mark bought a motorcycle in Virginia, and he made me wear extra layers of clothing when I rode on it. It was in the middle of the summer, and I had to wear jeans and a jean jacket before he would let me on because he was so worried about me getting injured in an accident and what my mother would say.

There was so much to explore in Mark's house. I felt so small yet significant there. The living room was more of a den with a TV and sofas and a bunch of movies. The kitchen was a big kitchen with a huge grandfather clock in the adjoined dining room. But the thing I remember most was the pantry, or the cupboard, however you call it. I guess the pantry and living room went hand-in-hand because the pantry held the snacks and drinks, and the living room held the entertainment. I walked in and looked up and all the shelves had been filled. The movie collection was what caught my attention first. I spent all day in there watching TV, either cable channels or one of the movies in the VHS collection. Little did I know that I would come to find what would become my favorite movie of all time: Ferris Bueller's Day Off. I have seen Ferris Bueller's Day Off so many times that I can say every line in the movie, verbatim, if you need me to do that for you for some reason. I know every line from Ferris, Sloan, Cameron, Jeannie, Mr. Rooney, Grace, Tom Bueller, Katie Bueller, etc. I can essentially ruin the movie for anyone.

Even though I love that movie, it is essentially about White Privilege, but the main character means well. If you haven't seen the movie, it's about a family who lives the American Dream in a Chicago suburb. The father is a marketing executive, and the mother is a real estate agent. They have two-point-two children in Ferris and Jeannie, who seem to be at each other's throats as teenagers and who attend the same predominantly white suburban high school. Perhaps they are a year apart, perhaps two. Ferris is an infamous prankster, and Jeannie is one of the antagonists in the movie, along with Mr. Rooney and Grace, who try to ruin his plan of skipping school, having adventures in Chicago, and getting away with it, yet again, like he always does.

Mark's family house was four or five times the size of Château Blasé. I wanted a house that big. I could have fit seven or eight of my house in that house. My trip to Mark's house in Fairfield included a trip to Manhattan, along with two stops in Newport, Rhode Island to visit his family, and Boston to see a Boston College vs. Harvard hockey game. Mark knew some friends who worked at Spin magazine, and we went to their offices and went out to eat and party. They gave me cassette tapes made for promotional release. I remember I had the new UMCs single Blue Cheese. I enjoyed New York City, and I appreciated it the whole entire few days that I was there. I saw the World Trade Center, FAO Schwarz, where I played on the foot-piano thing in the movie Big, and I stuck my hand in Guk. I went to the top of the Empire State Building and the Statue of Liberty on Staten Island. I looked for porn channels late at night, and we went out to eat and did things during the day. New York City and its shopping were meant for me, I concluded, but I had no money.

When I was younger, the thought of flying was what terrified me the most. I don't know if I would have ever flown anywhere else had I not taken my first flight to LaGuardia. I think I would have been just like my father, who had never been on an airplane until recently. I was scared of a lot of things when I was younger. I was far from being one of those brave souls who got on roller coasters or jumped into cold lakes and saw the exhilaration in doing things like that. The time that I went to Connecticut, I knew that I was going to be flying for the first time, and I was terrified. We flew from Dulles to LaGuardia, and it was only about a two-hour flight.

We drove from Charlottesville to Washington D.C. on the day of the flight. I had no idea about that which awaited me in the little city called Fairfield, Connecticut. I knew I had committed to taking an airplane and that it was Christmas time. This was going to be a two-week trip, and we had some more interesting places to see and things to do on the itinerary. This was the ultimate first-time experience in my life, and I was absolutely aware and unnerved every minute of being seven miles in the air. I was huddled beside Mark on my pioneering first flight. It was just a short skedaddle up the Atlantic coast. I still have the same uneasiness about flying because I don't like heights. Mark was the first person who I had ever heard use the words "turbulence" and "discombobulated", and he told me that turbulence was something you have to just accept as a part of flying. He said it was natural for a plane to experience turbulence. If there was one thing I was certain of then, it was that I was not even trying to be in a plane crash. No, I was not encouraged by any survivors I had heard of from past plane crashes. Although I had often pondered the slim chances of surviving something like that, Mark pretty much smothered that little murmur and breath of optimism by reassuring me that if the plane we happened to be on crashed to the Earth, that we would both die, and that would be that.

I actually helped Mark build a house in Vermont, too. Ralph Ellison said in an interview he did with the Paris Review in 1955 that he wrote the first paragraph of Invisible Man in Vermont. And he said that the history of the American Negro is a most intimate part of American history. And that through the very process of slavery came the building of the United States. And that Negro folklore, evolving within a larger culture that regarded it as inferior, was an especially courageous expression because it announced the Negro's willingness to trust his own experience, his own sensibilities as to the definition of reality, rather than allow his masters to define these crucial matters for him. It was after some time in China and Taiwan, which is where the money apparently was, that Mark and a friend of his bought some land in Irasburg, Vermont. I saw the town name only when I arrived. I remember Irasburg being a very small, Mayberry-like town from The Andy Griffith Show in the middle of mountainous nowhere. It was in the middle of Vermont ski country, where we had to rough it with no modern conveniences. That was one thing about Mark and most white people of that generation that I could never understand, and that was why were their lives so centered on experiencing things with only the bare essentials? I loved heat and spices in my food and other modern conveniences. All white people needed was a sleeping bag and a campfire to experience and get the essence of life. I was particularly whiny, too, so it took some time for me and Irasburg to click. The click occurred when I got behind the controls of the cat's claw and found out that I had a talent for digging ditches. Since then, I have dug myself into some pretty big ones, per se. The cat's claw made work easier like the cotton gin, and soon I was head of irrigation, sewage, and draining on the job site in Irasburg. I was precisely digging space for the pipes next to the house, and I was adroitly speculating rain and other erosion with ditches that led away from the structure for draining purposes. This was my thing, and I enjoyed getting up and starting the cat's claw every day.

Exeter's school motto of "non sibi" means not for self. Mark and Bill both knew Edmund Perry, who was a talented black student in their Exeter class who had been killed during a visit home to his native New York City after he and his older brother were said to have assaulted and robbed a plainclothes police officer. One day, while hanging out at Château Blasé, Mark and his roommates saw that the TV movie, Murder Without Motive: The Edmund Perry Story, was going to be airing later on in the week. He was very keen on me watching this film. This was such a current event for Mark because he had actually had some classes with Ed Perry. They were fellow Exonians, but Eddie was there on scholarship. Edmund Perry's opportunity out of his poor Harlem upbringing was education, yet the streets were his ultimate demise. This was also around the time when my older brothers were experimenting with various elements of street life.

Mark had a friend who was at UVA at the same time as him, and his name was Cornell. He sometimes called him "Sponell".

He sometimes called me "Little Spo". Coincidentally, a spo is a nickname for a guy who is a piece of shit, according to the Urban Dictionary. So, I guess it was a joke. If Ed Perry was the example of the black man who messed up his chance at making it in today's world, then Cornell was one of the success stories. I used to always think, "This guy talks like he is white." People always used to say that about me. But he sounded like that to me. His voice was blatantly nasal and articulate. Cornell went to Exeter with Mark, too. I did not really get into too many in-depth conversations with Cornell about what it was to be black at the University of Virginia because he was not one of the traditional black men that came to our schools during the school year. He was not a Kappa or an Omega or out in the field recruiting young African American students. He did not speak with the same slang. I distinctly remember him articulating the "t" when he said "What's up?" He didn't make it into a "z" sound like all the other regular black people. He did not wear his shirt tails over his waistline. He was a black that most people in my family would say "acted white". He did not have that particular swag. I sometimes would get called out for being this way by my classmates at school, but this was not true. I always used to wonder what people in my high school would have said about him because I knew they would laugh.

    My two older brothers were also my role models back then. They lived with their father and were inseparable. I used to emulate my oldest brother's handwriting and appreciated his phone manner when talking to girls. He was a star athlete in high school. My second oldest brother, Greg, I emulated as we both emulated George. Greg was a basketballer, football player, track team member, and wrestler in high school. George was the star wideout on the football team and the state champion in the 110-

meter hurdles. George was really my big brother, as in, the oldest. Even though George, Greg, and I didn't see each other daily, we saw each other twice a week during church.

George and Greg were products of my mother's first marriage to George, Sr. He was a semi-professional boxer who was either undefeated, or only lost one or two fights. He always tells me, halfway jokingly, how he used to beat my father. George and Greg and I are all two years apart in age, all spring and summer babies. I had the prettiest and curliest hair of us three; George was the oldest, and Greg was his sidekick, who says he has hair like me because there is "Indian" in his family, as in Native American. He doesn't. It is his favorite illusion he tells himself. Various knee injuries derailed their dreams of playing professional sports. They had the equal and opposite distinction of growing up with their father in the house but not with their mother. They were hardened by this process. I was just the opposite, as in overly sensitive to things. I cried a lot. I always sensed imminent doom. I could not control it. I would just cry. I am still that way to this day sometimes when I think about the past. I would cry if you stole from me, hit me too hard, or said something hurtful. It was too much work to get something back from someone who stole from me, I couldn't really fight that well, and I never really snapped back with some equally hurtful retort. All of my brothers and I have grown apart in recent years.

Mark's family and mine became inextricably linked, as he would gain the trust of my mother by safely and consistently getting me home at a decent hour and even helping her out of financial binds later in our siblingship, even though his parents and mine rarely communicated, as far I knew. I got the opportunity to go and live in France with a host family, thanks to Mark financing the trip. I went to Toulouse, France, and lived for a month with a cultural exchange program based in the same Vermont I had dug ditches in. I did The Experiment in International Living Program in Brattleboro, Vermont. This was another non-profit experience, but sponsored by World Learning. I had two new brothers and a new mother and father for the month. I got to apply the French I had been learning in high school. The family lived right outside of Toulouse, which then had the newest, most state-of-the-art metro system in the world. My two brothers were Ludovic and Florent. My new mom and dad were Maïté and Daniel. I enjoyed myself a lot in France then.

I was a part of a group of about fifteen students from all over the country who wanted to learn French in this type of immersion experience. When we first arrived, we spent a week in Paris, and then we were off to the South of France to meet our new families. We all met at Boston International Airport and got on a plane to Charles de Gaulle Airport. I knew to expect a slow pace of language and lifestyle and a nasal accent in the South of France and to expect rudeness and fast talkers in Paris. This was in all the textbooks.

My Experience as a Big Brother and My Time in San Francisco

I decided to volunteer as a Big Brother during my first couple of semesters at UVA to try and give back to this program that had played such an important role in how I saw my adult life up to that point. I had gotten into a few different schools, but I stayed home for my studies in a last-minute decision that I would honestly call cowardly in retrospect. But everything happens for a reason, they say. I got into UVA, Middlebury College, Oberlin College, and Kenyon College.

Oberlin was appealing because I had this video where Bill Cosby was narrating about the historical significance of Oberlin being the first college to accept African Americans. I applied to Kenyon College because I had heard they had some kind of reputed language program, and I knew I was going to study French. The same for Middlebury, but Middlebury's reputation for foreign languages seemed to be a little stronger than Kenyon's. I chose UVA in a last-minute haste because it was close to my neighborhood, and I hastily figured I could come home and eat, get money when I needed it, and enjoy the best of both worlds. I had already told the people at Oberlin College that I wanted to come there. Oberlin also had the Oberlin Conservatory for people who wanted to study music. Upon receiving a call from an admissions officer from Oberlin, I informed him at the last minute that I had changed my mind and decided to study at UVA. I felt really bad about that. I felt like I had let that guy down, and I could hear it in the disappointment in his voice. I was afraid to leave home.

At UVA, the townspeople are referred to as "townies", but I was both. A few of my high school friends also studied there. I knew the area and the neighborhoods around Charlottesville. I knew people at UVA and still had a few of my friends from my high school days who I hung out with. I had a foot in each world and always felt this added responsibility to represent both of them as much as I could. It vaulted me into a bourgeois feeling about my evolving place in the world. I knew that this kind of thing came with the territory, and I had nothing against thinking that way. It (was what W.E.B. Du Bois...) called "double-consciousness". It felt like what I was supposed to be doing. It felt like I was born to do that sort of thing. I was an upright guy. I was living and learning and earning, and I fairly questioned my motives and integrity often enough to consider myself valid and my efforts genuine enough to at least count for something. I had made plenty of mistakes at that point, and not being too critical of myself was a victory.

I had always felt like the "good guy" in my life, and that positive energy, that sense of knowing right from wrong, was my cursor. I knew where I was on my page all the time. I had a story, and I was the narrator. But I failed pretty miserably at my one attempt at being a Big Brother. I was matched with an eight-year-old named David, who also went to Jackson-Via Elementary. David was very shy, just like I used to be, during our first few encounters. He reminded me of me. He acted just like I acted during my first meetings with Mark. I was less timid with Bill and Kip because I had learned the ropes about that kind of thing. He was shyer than I was, or maybe it just looked that way because I was on the other side of the predicate nominative now.

However, I had been recently experimenting with marijuana and alcohol around this time and beginning my gradual descent into abuse of the two. I had a slowly deteriorating concept of reality and what it meant to be punctual, efficient, and generally prepared for what I was trying to cultivate myself for later in life: to become a French teacher. I had gotten this far on my ability alone but could not get the essence of what it took to succeed in university classes. When I was a Little Brother, I saw the people I met living life and managing responsibilities like it was the easiest thing in the world to do. Several times I saw Mark lying on his couch with his feet up, reading something assigned to him by a professor as he battled a hangover. I was pretty mortal when it came to focusing with a hangover. Some people can do that kind of thing. I couldn't do that back then. It didn't feel normal. Trying to balance my workload, drug and alcohol habits with going out and partying, a girlfriend, and my new buddy in the third grade was too much for my psyche because of the drugs and alcohol, even though I had been so familiar with that situation before. Bill was a pretty pensive and studious guy who was actually in law school when we were Big and Little Brothers. And Kip seemed to have all his stuff in order. From what I could see, all his ducks were in a row.

    I ended up getting put on academic probation after my third semester at UVA, then ultimately suspended for a year because I did not maintain a minimum grade point average. My relationship with David deteriorated after only a few months. I still feel bad about that. He was very shy, and I know I could have done more to establish more of a relationship with him, but I didn't. I used to often see his mother around town, but I never spoke to her. I always hope that she hasn't attached some villain status to me. I understand why if she has. Sometimes I used to keep silent out of shame when I saw her, and other times I doubted she remembered me. I had been part of a successful experience, and all of my Big Brothers actually honored their contracts with me, but I didn't really do enough to pay it forward. That thing that I had known to be such a precious relationship between two people from the best and worst of times was the same thing that I couldn't replicate for this little guy who came from my world. In my mind, I pretty much dropped the torch and started a wildfire with it. David came from a single parent household, just like I did, but I think he only had one sibling, a younger sister.

During my year of academic probation in my third year at UVA, Mark advised me to come and live in San Francisco, California, for my year off. I was very skeptical at first because I did not want to leave and be so far away from my mother, and San Francisco was notoriously filled with homosexuality. I had my doubts about living in such a place back then. It took a bit of convincing for me to believe that a change of environment was what I needed for a little while to get my head away from my failures at UVA. I left David and all of my other commitments behind in Virginia and took a detour in my quest; however, my substance abuse problem got worse in San Francisco. I had more resources to manage. I made a decent salary for an entry-level person, and it was more money than I had ever made before. I had a good job at a market research company, and I had a nice place to live in the heart of the Mission District in San Francisco. I had money to party. Mark was easily within reach right over in Potrero Hill. One of Mark's friends gave me a job in the production department of his company, which provided market research reports in the China Basin building. I was excited to start and prove myself in the working world. This same dude, Paddy, who owned the company, also had a younger brother in town who needed a roommate. I was new to town and had a job with his brother, so I was the perfect fit. Justin and I became buddies in no time!

The first thing I noticed about Paddy is that he was always working. He even told us he slept in his office sometimes. He rarely stopped working, yet he always found time to party. He always knew about a hip hop show somewhere in the city. Something was always happening at the Fillmore, or he knew about a cool bar somewhere in the Mission or Haight-Ashbury that played hip-hop music. I had never heard the name Padraic before, and that's Paddy's real name. Padraic or maybe Padraig. I don't quite remember exactly which it was on his diplomas.

Justin and I found a two-bedroom apartment in the Mission on Albion Street as it intersected with 16th Street. Justin was looking for a job. He specifically was on a mission to work at Banana Republic. Paddy also went to Exeter, and I had found a goldmine of a little network by the time I was twenty. It just kept getting better and more convenient. All these Exeter alumni kept making entrances. I kept finding out about all these new brothers I had in my life, and yet they were all white, except Cornell. Paddy and Justin also had another brother who had died a few years back. Occasionally they would share stories about their oldest brother, Colin. I'm glad they decided to let me into their sense of fraternity. I was glad I wasn't alone out there in California, and I felt safe while telling my parents about the new life I was leading. Unfortunately, Justin also passed away a couple of years ago because of a stroke. He was so young, and I was so shocked when I heard about it.

Justin was a little taller than Paddy, and he made a tall, goofy, and Ichabod Crane entry into my developing story in San

Francisco. I was a little jealous of Justin because he was the type of tall and blond surfer boy that attracted the tall, good-looking women that only the tall and blond men attract. He was a little older than me, particularly clumsy, and he was just a handsome dude. I actually enjoyed watching him work his maladroit magic with the ladies. It was pretty amusing watching him do his thing. Paddy also went to Harvard, just like Mark's older brother. Paddy studied the Classics, and I remember he had a little bookshelf full of books about ancient Greek civilization and philosophy. I asked him what he studied, and he said "The Classics," but I had no idea what he meant by that. I had seen that there was a Classics department at UVA, but I honestly had no clue what went on there or how practical a thing it was to study it or them, the Classics. Paddy also went to grad school at Harvard for business administration, hence him being the one who owned the company at which I got my first job. Mark studied economics at UVA and had a vested interest in Paddy because he was one of the initial investors in Paddy's company, Spins. Spins provided product sales information across various demographics in the United States. The company had found a way to track the sales of all the major brands in the Natural Products Industry, and to generate market reports according to the clients' specifications. When I worked at Spins, I learned about market research and about eating right. I even tried to be vegan for a while, something at which I failed miserably. Being vegan was too boring.

It was good to be on the scene in San Francisco, and I was enjoying myself out night after night, although spending too much money at bars and getting drunk. Part of this new, simpler Franciscan math was that, since more than half of the men in San Francisco were gay, I would have a better chance at getting women. This was true. I met many different people from all over the place. I went and visited old friends I had met through other camps and my exchange experience in France. I found a photographer girlfriend and a little crew of rapper dudes who loved the same music as I did. I developed a reputation at open mic nights around San Francisco and Marin County. I was such an initial hit on the Bay Area underground rap scene in my own little way that I came back to my hometown ready to make something happen with music. It was such a relief to get away from where I was raised for those nine months and all the dysfunction and absence. I felt so useless and hopeless trying to finish my homework assignments in Virginia then, yet San Francisco and that good entry-level job were so welcoming and perfect for reconstructing my self-confidence. And there were so many new and different women. It seemed like I had more than enough money to live during the day and party at night. Charlottesville's web didn't seem so inescapable. I did not make any money in California trying to do music, but I had a decent-paying job during the day and a well-established support system at my disposal a bus ride away in Potrero Hill. And the underground rap scene seemed like magic. It felt good to be creative. It felt therapeutic, however illogical drug and alcohol abuse were becoming.

Conversely, I was seeing a therapist about my depression concerning what my mission was in life. I was having trouble figuring that out. I would soon begin taking medication to counter the effects of my depressive episodes, which came to be diagnosed as full-blown medical chemical imbalances around this time. Mark even agreed to pay for my therapy sessions. All the drugs and alcohol tipped my psychological scales. I wouldn't start taking medication until I got back to Charlottesville, but Mark and I had conversations about it while I was in San

Francisco. He didn't see anything wrong with it, but I saw it as being a complete failure and some kind of admission that I was actually insane. I had failed in school at UVA, and I was seeing my therapist once a week, and I thought it was a good thing. I did not have to pay for it, so I figured I should go ahead and keep going. At $125 an hour, I was convinced that somehow it would work. It was 1999, and I partied the whole of it. I remember I had the choice to either stay and work in California because I actually had stock options at the job I had, or come back to Virginia and finish my degree in French. I chose to come back to Virginia and finish my degree. Had I stayed in California and worked for another three years, there would have been a bonus of $50,000 in my savings account to help me along the way into what would have been my first few years in life as a college graduate.

Instead of coming back and finishing my French degree, I got caught up even more in drugs and alcohol. It got even worse. I started experimenting with cocaine a few years after I got back. I drifted in and out of classes at UVA, completing what I could and coming up with money here and there from part-time jobs. For about seven years, I was sinking lower and lower into alcohol, marijuana, and cocaine abuse. I don't remember who exactly introduced me to cocaine, but once they did, I was hooked. I loved it. Mark was also sending me $500 per month for living expenses. He set up an automatic account for me to receive the money every month, and I used the money for things like rent, food, bills, etc. But I was getting way into cocaine then. I would hit a line and lean back to wait for the stupor to begin. I would do it again and again until the cocaine ran out, then again until all my money ran out for the month. Then another check would come, and I was good again. I had thought I would come back home, quickly finish my degree, maybe move back to San

Francisco and go back to the same company, and maybe even be qualified for a higher-paying position. I had very nice apartments, thanks to Mark's help and his signature as guarantor that I would meet any financial obligations. The way all my friends would come over and hang out until I eventually ended up with nothing was like déjà vu all over again, like the great Yogi Berra once said. Everybody came to my house to drink beer, listen to music, smoke weed, do cocaine, etc. I was living in a nice condo in the county, but I wound up having one of my several nervous breakdowns in life, and I had to be checked into the hospital for psychological examination and a couple of weeks' stay with other patients who had all types of psychiatric problems. Some of their faces were familiar from seeing them around town. I actually felt no shame when seeing the same people I had to share the same hospital floor with around town. I had to do the same thing in California one time because I decided to sit and smoke so much marijuana that it made me pass out after deciding to have a high adventure exploring around San Francisco. I remember going into a mall and feeling like the world was ending or the walls were caving in. I remember passing out and falling flat on my back and looking up, seeing four or five police officers checking my vital signs and asking me questions about who I was and where I was from. My mother actually came and got me from California on a plane with my brother George at what was a moment's notice when that happened. The fact that I wound up back in the hospital for the same psychological stuff was what began to alarm many people.

    I had to sit in the psychiatric ward at the University of Virginia hospital for about two weeks and smile and nod as I anticipated being let out so I could be free again. Several doctors during this time in my life suggested that I take antidepressants.

I was never comfortable with taking medications because I did not think that they were necessary. I didn't think it was a "natural" thing. I also thought that the world was so morally wrong across the board; how could it be me that needed medication? Why was I to blame? I was always ultimately lost in my own philosophical attempts to explain all that was wrong with the world, and the resounding theme that I heard from psychotherapists, guidance counselors, parents, and others versed in the words of the wise was that maybe I needed to slow down and simplify my life because drugs and alcohol had been accelerating my thoughts and influencing my decision-making into this whole detrimental mess. I suffered from clinical depression about the circumstances of my life, but I was also a genius with mild schizophrenia. It was a "good news, bad news" kind of thing. I was under the impression that I would never ever, ever find any sort of clarity, only this hazy continuity in my life, and that I would never ever, ever get it together because there was just entirely too much stuff going on inside my head. Both my mother and father seemed to let me just continue on my path in a respectful-of-boundaries sort of way. No one got too involved in my personal decisions, and only a couple of times could I sense frustration from them. They pretty much let me live and learn as life came at me then. Sometimes they would help me out with money and advice when they could, but toward the end of this episode in my life, their help and advice became mechanical and understandably devoid of any real emotion: they were just being my parents after a while. I think they both came to some realization that they each had done all they individually could, and all they could do was have faith that I would turn out okay. Besides, they had never been known to collectively intervene on my behalf anymore anyway.

I knew that I was approaching exhaustion while using drugs and alcohol, but I was convinced that I had not quite yet exhausted their effects. I saw a point in hallucination as a way to preserve myself and my vanishing. I found myself at rock bottom in the town I grew up in, even though I had had more than enough help to succeed. I had seen some significant stuff in my life up till then, too. It just didn't add up. I was doing the same thing every day. I was in the same places every day. I was seen the same way every day. I was wearing the same clothes several days in a row. Drugs and alcohol did not have the same high as they once had, although they did still technically impair me. When I did not have them, I was either thinking about getting them, trying to convince people to share theirs, or trying to scrape up enough money to buy some cheap beer and sit to ponder my demise while comfortably buzzed. I sat and waited for people to bring up the subjects of cocaine or hard liquor. I chose all the wrong friends. I chose all the wrong living situations. I identified with the wrong way of life. I did recognize, however, that no one should be living that way. I did not care how I looked, or how often I bathed, and I became comfortable with living the way I was living. I was comfortable with everyone else apparently aware that I was evidently going through something negative in my life.

Help From Some Friends

A friend of mine from UVA, along with her husband, noticed the negative turn that I had taken. One day, they asked me out of the blue if I would like to come and stay and live with them for a while to get back on my feet. The one condition was that I was not allowed to drink any alcohol and, naturally, no drugs either. As ingrained as I was in my way, I said OK. I was relieved but reluctant. I was relieved that someone else had decided to take a chance on me. I had been so invested in before, but I was so far gone recently that it was a real relief to see someone else who cared. I was reluctant because I had gotten used to the mechanics of drinking. I drank any kind of beer. I drank leftover beer. I drank warm beer. I had patience with frozen beer. I would drink any liquor: gin, bourbon, rum, vodka, Jägermeister, and any other liquor that was invented. I would drink any kind of wine, too.

    I knew that I was making drinking a gateway to other drugs. I knew that after a few drinks, I was open to doing harder drugs. I ended up doing drugs I told myself I would never do after I exhausted drinking. I had been drinking since I was eighteen, when I used to pay the older guys to go to the corner store and buy our drinks for us during my first year at UVA. All the male figures in my life drank. The University of Virginia "Wahoo" is a fish that can drink several times its weight in water. I was always playing it cool at Château Blasé while Mark and his friends drank. Mark never let me drink, though. One day he explained to me what he was doing by leaving the top off some apple cider on the sill in his kitchen window on Maury Avenue; he was letting the sugar in the cider ferment into alcohol. I drank with him in San Francisco, but never while he was an undergraduate. Neither Bill nor Kip let me drink with them either. Neither of them was big on drinking, not around me at least, as far as I could tell.

So, I ended up living with my two friends from UVA, who had both graduated and were recently married. They had just had a daughter yet welcomed me into their home in order for me to get myself back on my feet. They were living the life I was supposed to be living. I had a room to myself in their house, and all I had to do was agree to go to church once a week and stop drinking and doing drugs, something I could easily do. I was tired of drinking and doing drugs and not getting anywhere, and I knew I had a certain IQ for religion and church because I grew up in the church. The church they attended was sort of a mix between Presbyterian and Methodist. The church was predominantly white, and the congregation looked pretty wealthy as the building was more than accommodating and always advertising activities with other churches, programs for children, and international mission trips. The church even had a ministry in Haiti where they sent people every year to build houses and deliver other supplies and things to a small, underdeveloped community on the island. I was immediately optimistic about maybe being part of an international mission team because I had studied French.

While sitting among the congregation that first Sunday, I saw a different-looking group cast to the front left of the sanctuary. Most of them were black and some white. There was definitely a different dynamic to them. You could tell there were several leaders among them, like in a camp or some sort of overseen activity. You could see the hierarchy in the group and that they were a proctored group. The group, I would come to find out, was from The Bridge Ministry in a neighboring town.

The Bridge Ministry was a program for substance abusers or guys in prison who got a plea deal for lesser time if they agreed to go see this one man for lessons in leadership and re-acclimation back to living soberly. This guy had been a former drug dealer in my hometown, but after more than a decade in prison, he had gotten out and committed his life to ensure that as many men as possible would learn that there was no benefit in that lifestyle. To my chagrin, there would be no glamor of international ministry for me just yet. Little did I know that my two friends' plan for me was to go with these men and be a part of this program that helped addicts and people with other life-controlling issues get their lives back together. It was an eighteen-month commitment to which I, again reluctantly, agreed. It was the caveat that no one had told me about. So, after two months of going to church every Sunday, getting home cooking, and relevant, intelligent conversation, I was off to this program for eighteen months of spiritual basic training and a refresher course in life skills. I got on the ministry bus in 2007 one Sunday after church. I had packed my things earlier that morning, and now I was off to try and piece together my broken life like Chinua Achebe warned.

The Bridge was like a Christian boot camp. We woke up every morning around six. We cleaned our rooms and got showered and cleaned up for breakfast. After breakfast, we had a short church service every morning with worship hymns and an encouraging word for the day or a semi-scolding reprimand because of a mistake or mishap the day before. Every new person at the Bridge had to do a month's duty in the kitchen, where he either helped prepare the food or he cleaned up afterward. I only ended up doing two weeks in the kitchen before I was moved to coax data wire assembly and other appliance assembly for a company called National Optronics (owned by some French people) that had a small production center on the Bridge campus. I did feel at home in the kitchen, though. Everyone knew that I had gone to UVA, so I was ushered into the more cerebral assembly side of the campus. When there was no work to do there, I would join the yard crew and help clean up around the property. I met all kinds of people at the Bridge. All kinds of lifelong crooks and young misfits came in and out of that place. Some of them kept coming back after they were free to go. Some got kicked out. I met some guys that used to run the streets with my father.

The program helped mercurial men get their feet back on solid ground as they were often in and out of the prison system, something that was frowned on by a lot of potential employers. Fortunately for all of us, the Bridge had built a rapport with many construction, landscaping, and handyman companies in the area that welcomed the opportunity to have a hand in a man's rehabilitation. Jesus was a carpenter, right? The program has many friends and benefactors, including John Grisham, the author, and John Hornsby, Bruce Hornsby's brother.

After the twelve-month mark in the program, the pastor has a ceremony for you in front of friends, family, and other supporters and tells you in the form of a comprehensive analysis of what you did right and wrong and things you should work on in the future in your new life after you get back out into the world. If you were an exceptional participant and upstanding citizen for the length of the campus part, then you get invited to live at the Interim House, where the rent is cheap, so you can have six months to save some money to help you get back out there in the working world and be able to pay a few months of normal rent. I was invited to the Interim House for six months because I completed the program on the campus with success. I had successfully navigated through various jobs on the campus. I had gained about fifty pounds and was really looking like a man for the first time in a good little while. I didn't have any significant incidents or conflicts while I was there. I was pretty diligent and focused on everything in which I was involved. I was piecing stuff together, and day-to-day obligations and new opportunities made just a little more sense. And I was a "Responsible" in the program, a title given to the participants who displayed above-average leadership skills. Responsibles were put in charge to a certain degree to let other participants know of changes in protocol. We were liaisons to the administrative staff and Pastor Washington.

Once at the Interim House, I was made the House Manager, where I was again a liaison between the management of the program and the other members of the house. If house members got out of line, then I reported what they did to the higher-ups. If anything needed to be communicated to the house members by the higher-ups, a lot of the time I was the messenger. I got a sense of what it was to be a leader again, the leader that everyone predicted I would eventually become when I was in middle school and high school before I got derailed by my substance abuse. Now I could say that not only did I commit to reorganizing my priorities and getting my life back in order by kicking my substance abuse habits, I actually did it in a locally recognized context. I found that people in my community respected successful rehabilitation. I had put my best foot forward for eighteen months and come up with success. Although this was an unconventional victory, it was a major one because it was a victory in my spirit.

The Horse's Mouth

So now, here I am, and thirty-five years have passed since I raised my hand in my fourth-grade homeroom class when Mrs. Harding asked everyone if they would be interested in the Madison House Big Siblings Program. I have a little more clarity about my life circumstances after traveling around Europe and Eurasia for the past six years, learning different languages and learning about different cultures, especially in the former Yugoslavia and Soviet Union. Those regions fell apart so many years ago and have grown back into independent states with distinct identities, national pride, tourist attractions, and most importantly, a sense of optimism and a new trajectory in the world economy. Before I started traveling, I was living and working around Charlottesville waiting tables, doing survey research at the UVA sociology department research center, and doing general labor at a local temp agency that had a partnership with the rehabilitation program I went to. I wasn't doing much with French, other than a conversation group here and there and I presented a film or two at the Charlottesville French Film Festival. I had found an Italian conversation group to practice with and had also taken a couple of Chinese classes on the Downtown Mall. Learning different languages helps me medicate myself by studying something new so I don't feel so bridled by English and the legacy of the American system.

When I raised my hand in Mrs. Harding's class, I knew what it meant, and I was fully aware of what I was doing as she invited us through that curtain into the dressage of university life. I put myself and my family in the hotseat and I requested intercession. I always had a sense of hope about my family and was secure about my role in our clan, but I was seeking mentorship because my father wasn't in my everyday life. So many people had already been pointing me in the right direction at even that young age, and I had been shielded from a lot of bad stuff in life because little white lies aren't so bad every once in a while. The Quest program had invited me to think critically about things and to always question the order of our world so that I wouldn't lose my head and blame myself. My obedient nature and knack for French took me to the University of Virginia, where I became a bit of a lush and a hayburner, and had to swallow my pride after two years of academic mediocrity and accept academic suspension for a year, and hope that all my teachers telling me I was a gifted student wasn't one of those little white lies.

The concrete reality that my mother had made upward mobility for me while growing up in America's invisible hand economics was really very new and just under my feet. My acceptance into UVA was a sense of hope for my family. It was a proper distinction given our involvement in street ministry and the positive example my mother set for my younger brother and I with prayer and fasting, constantly improving our standard of living year by year. With her guiding our reins, we went from living in the projects to home ownership in less than ten years due to whatever spurred her. I started the Big Siblings program a couple of years before we owned our first house. All my teachers expected me to go to college and continue my education. It was certainly going to be French that I studied because I was among the top students in Virginia.

All my Big Brothers represented a source of credibility for me while growing up. I could cross-reference all of my experiences with them for a greater sense of confidence and people skills. It was empowering to share my thoughts and opinions with those adults, and to be taken seriously as an adolescent, and to be in the saddle as it pertained to my destiny. It validated everything as I got treated like an intellectual equal. I felt like part of a tandem with each of my Big Brothers. The American legal system and all the nation's intellectuals saw the Taney Court ride roughshod over Dred Scott's suit for manumission in 1857, denying Scott's suit had merit based on "diversity of citizenship" because no African descendant could claim citizenship. And the American literary community saw Harper Lee make Atticus Finch a hero in accepting Tom Robinson's case in To Kill A Mockingbird, despite the threat of the mob from the Maycomb locals to Atticus and his family while he puts his neck on the line for Tom. The more and more we come together racially, the more possibilities we have for a better community.

Charlottesville is my American hometown in the Mother of States and Old Dominion that stands out among other hometowns as so seminal to American political thought, where Madison House is a great little corner of the American social experiment. I exited my American hometown in the state also known as the Mother of Presidents on the Atlantic coast, down where the South begins, where my mother used to make me sit on her feet while she did sit-ups. I just left one day because I decided to leave before the ground beneath my feet completely broke. The internet was my periscope and I decided to try my hand at being groundbreaking in my own solitary way, and I outran the bias and tawny and tree bark smell of my hometown's books and began to see the world for myself. I, still not so long in the tooth, took a bite out of the Earth's red delicious geography, past the so-called excellence of that literary era so conveniently coupled with African enslavement and the Antebellum American South.

It's no accident that those things from the Orient in our living room growing up and the old Russia and Soviet Union I heard about in the news when I was young have so much to do with my life today as an African descendant of generations of free labor. The lure of capitalism and laissez-faire and the pull of the suspiciously cognate communism and community created a vertigo throughout my childhood where a lot of my baited optimism went to die. The American economy never really made sense and all the black kids knew the consequences of disobeying the slavemaster, and progress for us was always two steps forward and one step back. The picture of Russia and the old Soviet Union was of "a barren field covered with snow", to quote from Langston Hughes's poem "Dreams", while the only ones who mattered in the United States were typically "older, white, and somewhat more free", to quote from another of Hughes's poems, "Theme For English B".

I've stretched my childhood myopia into a noble analysis, searching to understand just what the opportunity cost was of growing up black in the United States, and I can be a ghost of and to my past and try to recoup some of it. People must keep facing social injustice and the legacy of disenfranchisement like in the Komunyakaa poem, "Facing It", about the trauma and aftereffects of war. We must look up and face it. We must make more of an attempt to answer this hideously loaded question. Living and working around the world as a digital nomad has required poise in different situations, as traveling while black has its challenges. Calling Madison House a saving grace is no overestimation, and I think I've kept my marbles because of it, but there certainly is a pressure in synopsizing it. I personally hit the jackpot with the breadth of experiences and characters I met along the way. All the stories are probably not like mine. Life has been a long, strange trip about living and learning as a world citizen, while the tension in Sino-American relations has the world on the verge of a new number one economy. I am interested to see if my skills I have learned will serve me well and keep me relevant in our changing world until all of humanity's iniquities and inequities have been counted.